Cloud Computing With Python For Beginners

A Comprehensive Guide To Building
Scalable Cloud Applications Using Essential
Frameworks

Bronson E. Lee

Table Of Content

DISCLAIMER

The authors and publishers of "Cloud Computing With Python For Beginners" have diligently striven to ensure the accuracy and completeness of the information contained within this book at the time of publication. However, it is crucial to acknowledge that the field of software development, including Cloud Computing, is characterized by rapid advancements and evolving best practices.

Therefore, the authors and publishers offer no warranty, express or implied, regarding the enduring accuracy, completeness, suitability, or effectiveness of the information presented herein. Readers are strongly encouraged to remain abreast of the latest developments in Cloud Computing, associated technologies, and industry best practices through continued learning and engagement with relevant resources.

The authors and publishers shall not be held liable for any errors, omissions, or any losses or damages of any kind arising from the use of, or reliance upon, the information contained within this book. This includes, but is not limited to, incidental, consequential, or punitive damages.

The code examples provided in this book are intended for illustrative purposes only and may necessitate modification to suit specific applications or environments. The reader assumes full responsibility for the implementation and consequences of utilizing any code, techniques, or methodologies described herein.

All trademarks, trade names, and logos mentioned in this book are the property of their respective owners. Any references to third-party resources, websites, or materials are provided for convenience and informational purposes only. The authors and publishers do not endorse or assume any responsibility for the content, accuracy, or availability of such external resources.

By utilizing the information presented in this book, the reader acknowledges and agrees to the terms of this disclaimer.

INTRODUCTION

Welcome to the exciting world of cloud computing with Python! This book is your comprehensive guide to embarking on a journey that will equip you with the knowledge and skills to build scalable and efficient cloud applications. Whether you're a budding developer, an IT professional seeking to expand your expertise, or simply curious about the power of the cloud, this book will provide you with a solid foundation and practical guidance.

Why Cloud Computing with Python?

Cloud computing has revolutionized the way we develop, deploy, and manage applications. It offers unparalleled scalability, flexibility, and cost-effectiveness, allowing businesses and individuals to access on-demand computing resources without the burden of managing infrastructure. Python, with its versatility, readability, and extensive ecosystem of libraries and frameworks, has become a language of choice for cloud development. Its simplicity and power make it an ideal tool for building everything from simple web applications to complex data processing pipelines and machine learning models in the cloud.

What You Will Learn:

This book takes a hands-on approach to learning, guiding you through the essential concepts and practical skills needed to build cloud applications with Python. You will:

- **Gain a solid understanding of cloud computing fundamentals:** Explore the core concepts of cloud computing, its benefits, and the different service models (IaaS, PaaS, SaaS).
- **Master essential Python skills for cloud development:** Learn the fundamental Python concepts relevant to cloud development, including data types, control flow, functions, and modules.
- **Dive deep into core cloud services:** Explore compute services (VMs, containers, serverless), storage services (object storage, databases), and networking fundamentals (VPCs, subnets, security).
- **Build web applications with popular Python frameworks:** Learn how to use Flask, Django, and FastAPI to create web applications and deploy them to the cloud.
- **Create and consume APIs:** Understand how to design and build RESTful APIs and integrate with external APIs in your applications.

- **Explore advanced cloud topics:** Delve into security best practices, scalability and performance optimization, and monitoring and logging techniques.
- **Gain practical experience with real-world projects:** Apply your knowledge to build practical projects, such as a to-do list application, an e-commerce platform, or a machine learning model deployment.

Who Should Read This Book:

This book is designed for beginners with little to no prior experience in cloud computing or Python. Whether you're a student, a hobbyist, or a professional seeking to transition to cloud development, this book will provide you with the necessary foundation and practical guidance.

How This Book Is Organized:

This book is structured to guide you through a progressive learning journey:

- **Part I: Foundations:** Lays the groundwork with introductions to cloud computing and essential Python concepts.
- **Part II: Core Cloud Services:** Explores the fundamental building blocks of cloud

infrastructure, including compute, storage, and networking.

- **Part III: Building Cloud Applications:** Dives into web development with Python frameworks, API creation and consumption, and microservices.
- **Part IV: Advanced Topics and Best Practices:** Covers essential security practices, performance optimization techniques, and monitoring and logging strategies.

Your Capstone Project and MSSQL:

As you mentioned this book will contribute to your capstone project, it's worth noting that while the book covers a broad range of cloud concepts and Python techniques, you can certainly tailor your learning and project implementation to align with your specific goals. Regarding your use of Microsoft SQL Server Management Studio (MSSMS), remember that the core database concepts and SQL skills you acquire are transferable across different database systems. While specific syntax and tools might vary, the foundational knowledge you gain will be invaluable.

Embark on Your Cloud Journey:

We encourage you to approach this book with a curious mind and a willingness to experiment. Cloud computing is a dynamic and ever-evolving field, and continuous learning is key to staying ahead of the curve. With dedication and practice, you'll be well on your way to building robust, scalable, and innovative cloud applications with Python. Let's begin!

Part I: Foundations of Cloud Computing with Python

Chapter 1: Introduction to Cloud Computing

What is Cloud Computing?

Imagine this: you need powerful computers, vast storage, and sophisticated software to run your business. But instead of buying and managing all that yourself, you simply rent it online from a company that specializes in these things. That's the core idea behind cloud computing. It's a modern approach to information technology where you access a shared pool of resources like servers, storage, databases, and software over the internet. These resources reside in enormous data centers owned by companies called cloud providers, the biggest names being Amazon Web Services (AWS), Microsoft Azure, and Google Cloud Platform (GCP).

This means no more huge investments in physical hardware or complex software installations. You get exactly what you need, precisely when you need it, and pay only for the time you use it. This makes businesses of any size nimble, cost-effective, and able to grow quickly.

Defining Features of Cloud Computing:

- **Self-Service on Demand:** You're in control. Get the computing resources you require instantly, without needing to go through a lengthy process with the provider.
- **Access from Anywhere:** As long as you have an internet connection, you can access cloud services from any device, whether it's your laptop, phone, or tablet.
- **Shared Resources:** The provider's powerful hardware isn't dedicated to just one customer. It's pooled to serve many clients efficiently, with resources allocated dynamically based on demand.
- **Flexibility and Scalability:** Need more power? Cloud resources can be scaled up or down automatically and instantly to match your exact needs at any given moment.
- **Usage-Based Billing:** No more guessing games with IT costs. Cloud services are metered, so you pay only for the resources you actually consume.

A Helpful Analogy: Think of cloud computing like the electricity grid. You don't need to build your own power plant to enjoy the benefits of electricity. You simply plug into the existing grid and pay for what you use. Similarly, cloud computing lets you tap into a vast network of computing power without the hassle of owning and maintaining the infrastructure.

Why Cloud Computing Matters:

- **Reduced Costs:** Say goodbye to hefty upfront investments in hardware and software. Cloud computing shifts your expenses from capital expenditure to a more manageable operational expense.
- **Effortless Scalability:** Growing your business or facing a sudden surge in demand? Cloud computing makes it easy to scale your resources up or down to meet your needs.
- **Unmatched Flexibility:** Access your data and applications from anywhere in the world, at any time, empowering your workforce and streamlining operations.
- **Increased Reliability:** Cloud providers offer robust infrastructure with built-in redundancy and disaster recovery, ensuring your business stays online even in challenging situations.
- **Enhanced Security:** Leading cloud providers invest heavily in security measures to protect your valuable data from threats.
- **Focus on Innovation:** Free your IT team from the burden of managing infrastructure. Cloud computing allows them to focus on

developing innovative solutions that drive your business forward.

Cloud Computing in the Real World:

- **Streaming your favorite shows:** Services like Netflix rely on cloud computing to deliver seamless streaming experiences to millions of viewers worldwide.
- **Storing your memories:** Platforms like Google Photos utilize cloud storage to keep your photos and videos safe and accessible.
- **Working together seamlessly:** Tools like Google Docs enable real-time collaboration on documents stored in the cloud, boosting productivity and teamwork.
- **Powering businesses:** Applications like Salesforce, a leading Customer Relationship Management (CRM) platform, are entirely cloud-based.

Cloud Computing vs. Traditional IT:

Feature	Traditional IT	Cloud Computing
Infrastructure	You own and maintain it	Managed by the provider
Cost	High upfront investment	Pay-as-you-go, like a utility

Scalability	Difficult and slow to adjust	Easy and instant scaling
Accessibility	Usually limited to your physic'ocation	Access from anywhere with nternet
Maintenance	Requires your own dedicated IT staf	Handled by the provider

In Conclusion:

Cloud computing is reshaping how we use technology in business and everyday life. By offering readily available, shared computing resources, it brings numerous advantages. As you progress through this book, you'll gain a deeper understanding of cloud concepts and learn how to harness its power to build and deploy your own applications.

Benefits of Cloud Computing

Cloud computing offers a compelling array of benefits that have made it a transformative force in the world of IT. Let's delve deeper into some of the key advantages that make the cloud an attractive option for businesses and individuals alike:

1. Cost Savings:

One of the most significant benefits of cloud computing is its potential for substantial cost savings. By shifting from a capital expenditure (CapEx) model to an operational expenditure (OpEx) model, you can significantly reduce your IT costs. Here's how:

- **Reduced upfront investment:** You no longer need to invest heavily in expensive hardware like servers, storage devices, and networking equipment. The cloud provider takes care of the infrastructure, allowing you to avoid significant upfront costs.
- **Pay-as-you-go pricing:** Cloud services typically operate on a pay-as-you-go model, meaning you only pay for the resources you consume. This eliminates the need to overprovision resources to accommodate peak demand, resulting in significant cost savings.
- **Lower operating costs:** Cloud providers handle the maintenance and management of the infrastructure, reducing the need for in-house IT staff and associated costs.

2. Scalability and Flexibility:

Cloud computing offers unparalleled scalability and flexibility, allowing you to adapt to changing business needs quickly and efficiently.

- **On-demand scaling:** You can easily scale your resources up or down in response to fluctuating demand. This ensures that you have the right amount of computing power at any given time, avoiding performance bottlenecks or wasted resources.
- **Dynamic resource allocation:** Cloud platforms dynamically allocate resources based on your needs, ensuring optimal performance and cost efficiency.
- **Geographic reach:** Cloud providers have data centers located around the globe, enabling you to deploy your applications and services closer to your customers, improving performance and reducing latency.

3. Increased Efficiency:

Cloud computing can significantly improve your organization's efficiency by streamlining operations and automating tasks.

- **Focus on core business:** By offloading infrastructure management to the cloud provider, your IT team can focus on strategic initiatives and innovation, rather than day-to-day maintenance.

- **Improved collaboration:** Cloud-based tools and applications facilitate collaboration among teams, regardless of their location.
- **Automation:** Cloud platforms offer automation capabilities that can streamline tasks, reduce manual effort, and improve efficiency.

4. Enhanced Security:

While security concerns were once a barrier to cloud adoption, leading cloud providers now invest heavily in security measures to protect their customers' data.

- **Data encryption:** Cloud providers use encryption to protect data both in transit and at rest, safeguarding it from unauthorized access.
- **Access control:** Robust access control mechanisms ensure that only authorized users can access your data and applications.
- **Compliance certifications:** Cloud providers comply with various security and privacy standards, such as ISO 27001 and SOC 2, giving you confidence in their security posture.

5. Increased Reliability and Availability:

Cloud providers offer high availability and disaster recovery capabilities, ensuring that your applications and data are always accessible.

- **Redundancy:** Cloud infrastructure is designed with redundancy in mind, with multiple data centers and availability zones to ensure continuous operation even in the event of hardware failures or natural disasters.
- **Data backup and recovery:** Cloud providers offer data backup and recovery services, allowing you to quickly restore your data in case of data loss or corruption.
- **Disaster recovery:** Cloud-based disaster recovery solutions enable you to quickly recover your applications and data in the event of a major outage.

6. Fostering Innovation:

Cloud computing provides a platform for innovation, enabling you to experiment with new technologies and develop cutting-edge solutions.

- **Access to the latest technologies:** Cloud providers offer a wide range of services and tools, including artificial intelligence (AI), machine learning (ML), and the Internet of Things (IoT), empowering you to innovate and stay ahead of the curve.

- **Agile development:** Cloud platforms support agile development methodologies, enabling you to rapidly develop and deploy new applications and services.
- **Reduced time to market:** Cloud computing can help you bring your products and services to market faster, gaining a competitive advantage.

In conclusion, the benefits of cloud computing are numerous and far-reaching. By embracing the cloud, businesses and individuals can unlock new levels of efficiency, scalability, and innovation, while reducing costs and enhancing security.

Cloud Service Models (IaaS, PaaS, SaaS)

Cloud computing isn't a one-size-fits-all solution. It offers various service models to cater to different needs and levels of control. These models are often visualized as a stack, with each layer building upon the one below it. The three primary cloud service models are:

1. Infrastructure as a Service (IaaS):

IaaS provides you with the foundational building blocks of cloud computing. You get access to fundamental IT resources like virtual machines, storage, networking, and operating systems. Think of it as renting the raw materials to build your own IT infrastructure in the cloud.

What you get:

- **Virtual machines:** On-demand computing power in the form of virtual servers.
- **Storage:** Scalable and reliable storage options for your data.
- **Networking:** Virtual networks, subnets, and firewalls to connect your resources.
- **Operating systems:** A choice of operating systems to run on your virtual machines.

What you manage:

- **Operating systems:** You're responsible for configuring and managing the operating systems on your virtual machines.
- **Middleware:** You need to install and manage any middleware components required for your applications.
- **Runtime environments:** You're responsible for setting up and managing the runtime environments for your applications.

- **Applications:** You deploy, manage, and monitor your applications.

Examples:

- Amazon Elastic Compute Cloud (EC2)
- Microsoft Azure Virtual Machines
- Google Compute Engine

Use cases:

- Hosting websites and web applications
- Running development and testing environments
- Data storage and backup
- High-performance computing

2. Platform as a Service (PaaS):

PaaS takes things a step further by providing a complete platform for developing, deploying, and managing applications. You get all the infrastructure components of IaaS, plus additional tools and services that simplify application development and deployment. Think of it as renting a fully equipped workshop where you can focus on building your applications without worrying about the underlying infrastructure.

What you get:

- **Everything in IaaS:** Virtual machines, storage, networking, and operating systems.
- **Middleware:** Pre-configured middleware components like web servers, application servers, and databases.
- **Runtime environments:** Managed runtime environments for various programming languages and frameworks.

What you manage:

- **Applications:** You develop, deploy, and manage your applications.
- **Data:** You're responsible for managing your application data.

Examples:

- AWS Elastic Beanstalk
- Microsoft Azure App Service
- Google App Engine

Use cases:

- Building and deploying web applications
- Developing and testing software
- Running data analytics and machine learning workloads

3. Software as a Service (SaaS):

SaaS delivers software applications over the internet, on demand. You simply access and use the software through a web browser or mobile app, without worrying about any underlying infrastructure or software management. Think of it as subscribing to a service that provides you with the finished product, ready to use.

What you get:

- **Fully functional software applications:** Ready-to-use software applications accessible through a web browser or mobile app.
- **Automatic updates:** The software is automatically updated and maintained by the provider.
- **User support:** The provider typically offers user support and training.

What you manage:

- **User accounts:** You manage user accounts and access permissions.
- **Data:** You're responsible for managing your application data.

Examples:

- Salesforce

- Google Workspace (Gmail, Google Docs, Google Drive)
- Microsoft 365 (Word, Excel, PowerPoint)

Use cases:

- Customer relationship management (CRM)
- Email and collaboration
- Productivity applications
- Human resources management (HRM)

Choosing the Right Cloud Service Model:

The choice of cloud service model depends on your specific needs and requirements. Consider the following factors:

- **Control:** IaaS offers the most control, while SaaS offers the least.
- **Flexibility:** PaaS and SaaS offer greater flexibility than IaaS.
- **Cost:** SaaS is often the most cost-effective option for standardized applications.

By understanding the different cloud service models, you can choose the one that best aligns with your business objectives and technical capabilities.

Chapter 2: Python Essentials for Cloud Development

Data Types and Variables

In the world of programming, data is king. Whether you're building a web application, analyzing data, or training a machine learning model, you'll be working with different types of data. Python, being a versatile and dynamic language, offers a rich set of data types to represent and manipulate various kinds of information. Understanding these data types is crucial for writing effective and efficient Python code for cloud development.

What are Data Types?

A data type defines the kind of value a variable can hold and the operations that can be performed on it. It essentially categorizes data based on its characteristics. For instance, numbers, text, and true/false values all have distinct data types in Python.

Common Data Types in Python:

Python provides several built-in data types, each serving a specific purpose:

1. **Numeric Types:**
   - **Integers** (`int`): Represent whole numbers, both positive and negative (e.g., 10, -5, 0).
   - **Floating-point numbers** (`float`): Represent numbers with decimal points (e.g., 3.14, -2.5, 0.0).
   - **Complex numbers** (`complex`): Represent numbers with a real and imaginary part (e.g., 2 + 3j).
2. **Text Type:**
   - **Strings** (`str`): Represent sequences of characters enclosed in single or double quotes (e.g., "Hello", 'Python').
3. **Boolean Type:**
   - **Booleans** (`bool`): Represent truth values, either `True` or `False`.
4. **Sequence Types:**
   - **Lists** (`list`): Ordered, mutable collections of items (e.g., [1, 2, 'apple']).
   - **Tuples** (`tuple`): Ordered, immutable collections of items (e.g., (1, 2, 'apple')).
   - **Ranges** (`range`): Represent a sequence of numbers (e.g., `range(1, 5)` generates 1, 2, 3, 4).
5. **Mapping Type:**

- Dictionaries (`dict`): Unordered collections of key-value pairs (e.g., {'name': 'John', 'age': 30}).

6. **Set Types:**
   - **Sets** (`set`): Unordered collections of unique items (e.g., {1, 2, 3}).
   - **Frozen sets** (`frozenset`): Immutable versions of sets.

7. **None Type:**
   - `None`: Represents the absence of a value.

What are Variables?

Variables are like containers that hold data in your program. They are named locations in memory where you can store values of different data types. You can think of them as labels you assign to specific data.

Declaring and Assigning Variables:

In Python, you declare a variable by simply assigning a value to it:

Python

```
name = "Alice"     # Assigns the string "Alice" to the variable 'name'
```

```
age = 30        # Assigns the integer 30 to
the variable 'age'
price = 19.99   # Assigns the float 19.99
to the variable 'price'
```

Variable Naming Rules:

- Variable names must start with a letter (a-z, A-Z) or an underscore (_).
- The rest of the name can contain letters, numbers, and underscores.
- Variable names are case-sensitive (e.g., `name` and `Name` are different variables).
- Choose descriptive names that reflect the purpose of the variable.

Type Inference:

Python is dynamically typed, meaning you don't need to explicitly specify the data type of a variable. Python infers the type based on the value assigned to it.

Python

```
x = 10        # x is inferred as an integer
y = "Hello"   # y is inferred as a string
```

Type Conversion:

You can convert a variable from one data type to another using type conversion functions:

Python

```
x = 10
y = float(x)   # Converts x to a float (y
will be 10.0)

z = "20"
w = int(z)    # Converts z to an integer (w
will be 20)
```

Why are Data Types Important in Cloud Development?

- **Data Integrity:** Ensuring that data is stored and processed in the correct format.
- **Efficient Operations:** Using appropriate data types for optimal performance.
- **API Interactions:** Communicating with cloud APIs that expect data in specific formats.

- **Data Analysis:** Analyzing and interpreting data from cloud services.
- **Code Readability:** Making your code easier to understand and maintain.

Understanding data types and variables is fundamental to programming in Python. By mastering these concepts, you'll be well-equipped to handle data effectively in your cloud development projects.

Control Flow and Loops

In the realm of programming, instructions typically execute sequentially, one after the other. However, real-world scenarios often demand more dynamic behavior. This is where control flow comes into play. Control flow allows you to dictate the order in which instructions are executed, enabling your programs to make decisions, repeat actions, and respond to different conditions. Loops, a fundamental aspect of control flow, provide the power to execute a block of code repeatedly, making your programs more efficient and capable of handling repetitive tasks.

Conditional Statements:

Conditional statements allow your program to execute different blocks of code based on certain conditions. The most common conditional statement in Python is the `if-else` statement:

Python

```
age = 20

if age >= 18:
  print("You are an adult.")
else:
  print("You are a minor.")
```

In this example, the program checks if the `age` variable is greater than or equal to 18. If the condition is true, it prints "You are an adult." Otherwise, it prints "You are[1] a minor."

You can also use `elif` (short for "else if") to check multiple conditions:

Python

```
score = 85

if score >= 90:
  print("A")
elif score >= 80:
  print("B")
```

```
elif score >= 70:
  print("C")
else:
  print("D")
```

Loops:

Loops enable you to execute a block of code repeatedly. Python offers two main types of loops:

1. `for` **loop:**
   - Used to iterate over a sequence (e.g., a list, tuple, string, or range).
   - Executes the code block once for each item in the sequence.

Python

```
fruits = ["apple", "banana", "cherry"]

for fruit in fruits:
  print(fruit)
```

This code will print each fruit in the `fruits` list.

2. `while` **loop:**
   - ○ Used to repeat a block of code as long as a condition is true.
   - ○ The condition is checked before each iteration.

Python

```python
count = 0

while count < 5:
  print(count)
  count += 1
```

This code will print the numbers from 0 to 4.

Loop Control Statements:

- `break`: Terminates the loop prematurely.
- `continue`: Skips the current iteration and proceeds to the next.
- `pass`: Does nothing; used as a placeholder in loops or conditional statements.

Nested Loops:

You can nest loops within each other to create more complex iterations:

Python

```python
for i in range(3):
  for j in range(2):
    print(f"({i}, {j})")
```

This code will print all combinations of i and j.

Why are Control Flow and Loops Important in Cloud Development?

- **Automating tasks:** Loops are essential for automating repetitive tasks, such as processing large datasets or interacting with cloud APIs.
- **Data processing:** Control flow allows you to filter, transform, and analyze data from cloud services.
- **Conditional execution:** Conditional statements enable your programs to respond to different events and conditions in the cloud environment.

- **Building dynamic applications:** Control flow and loops are crucial for creating dynamic and interactive cloud applications.

By mastering control flow and loops, you gain the power to write more efficient, flexible, and sophisticated Python code for your cloud development projects.

Functions and Modules

As your Python code grows in complexity, it becomes essential to organize it into reusable and manageable chunks. This is where functions and modules come into play. Functions allow you to encapsulate a block of code that performs a specific task, making your code more modular and easier to read. Modules, on the other hand, enable you to group related functions and variables into separate files, promoting code reusability and organization across different projects.

Functions:

A function is a block of code that performs a specific task and can be called from other parts of your program. Functions[1] promote code reusability, reduce redundancy, and make your code more organized and maintainable.

Defining a Function:

In Python, you define a function using the `def` keyword, followed by the function name, parentheses, and[2] a colon:

Python

```
def greet(name):
    """This function greets the person passed
in as a parameter."""
    print(f"Hello, {name}!")

greet("Alice")  # Calling the function with
the argument "Alice"
```

This code defines a function called `greet` that takes a `name` as input and prints a greeting message. The `"""..."""` is a docstring, providing a description of the function's purpose.

Parameters and Arguments:

- **Parameters:** Variables listed inside the parentheses in the function definition. They act as placeholders for values that will be passed to the function when it's called.

- **Arguments:** The actual values passed to the function when it's called.

Return Values:

Functions can also return values using the `return` statement:

Python

```python
def add(x, y):
    """This function adds two numbers and
returns the sum."""
    return x + y

result = add(5, 3)   # Calling the function
and storing the result
print(result)   # Output: 8
```

Modules:

A module is a file containing Python definitions and statements. Modules allow you to organize your code into separate files, making it easier to manage and reuse.[3]

Importing Modules:

You can import modules using the `import` statement:

Python

```
import math

result = math.sqrt(25)    # Using the sqrt
function from the math module
print(result)   # Output: 5.0
```

This code imports the `math` module, which provides mathematical functions. You can then access functions from the module using the dot notation (e.g., `math.sqrt`).

Creating Modules:

You can create your own modules by simply saving your Python code in a file with a `.py` extension. You can then import this module into other Python scripts.

Why are Functions and Modules Important in Cloud Development?

- **Code organization:** Functions and modules help structure your cloud applications, making them more manageable and maintainable.
- **Code reusability:** You can reuse functions and modules across different parts of your application or even in different projects.
- **Abstraction:** Functions hide implementation details, allowing you to focus on the higher-level logic of your cloud application.
- **Collaboration:** Modules enable teams to work on different parts of a cloud project independently.
- **Maintainability:** Modular code is easier to update and modify without affecting other parts of the application.

By leveraging functions and modules effectively, you can write cleaner, more organized, and more maintainable Python code for your cloud development endeavors.

Chapter 3: Choosing Your Cloud Provider

AWS: Amazon Web Services

When it comes to cloud computing, Amazon Web Services (AWS) stands out as a dominant force. Since its inception in 2002, AWS has evolved into a comprehensive and widely adopted cloud platform, offering a vast and diverse range of services from its numerous data centers located across the globe. From agile startups to established Fortune 500 companies and government agencies, millions of customers rely on AWS to power their applications, drive innovation, and achieve cost efficiencies.

What Makes AWS a Leader:

- **Breadth and Depth of Services:** AWS provides the most mature and extensive collection of cloud services available, with over 200 fully featured offerings. These services encompass a wide spectrum of functionalities, including compute, storage, databases, analytics, networking, mobile, developer tools, and more.
- **Global Infrastructure:** With a vast global infrastructure comprising multiple regions and availability zones, AWS ensures

low-latency access to its services from virtually any location worldwide.

- **Commitment to Innovation:** AWS consistently pushes the boundaries of cloud technology, regularly introducing new services and features that enable customers to leverage cutting-edge advancements such as artificial intelligence (AI), machine learning (ML), and serverless computing.
- **Cost Optimization:** AWS employs a pay-as-you-go pricing model with competitive rates, empowering you to optimize your cloud expenditure and pay only for the resources you actually consume.
- **Unwavering Security:** AWS places a strong emphasis on security, providing a robust security framework and a diverse range of security services to help you safeguard your valuable data and applications.
- **Thriving Community and Ecosystem:** AWS fosters a vibrant and engaged community of users and developers, offering a wealth of resources, support, and expertise to its customers.

Exploring Core AWS Services:

Let's delve into some of the core AWS services that constitute the foundation of its cloud platform:

- **Compute:**
  - ○ **Amazon Elastic Compute Cloud (EC2):** This service delivers resizable compute capacity in the cloud, allowing you to launch virtual machines with a variety of operating systems and configurations tailored to your specific needs.
  - ○ **AWS Lambda:** This service enables serverless computing, empowering you to run code without the burden of provisioning or managing servers.
  - ○ **Amazon Elastic Container Service (ECS) and Amazon Elastic Kubernetes Service (EKS):** These services facilitate the deployment and management of containerized applications, enabling you to operate containers at scale.
- **Storage:**
  - ○ **Amazon Simple Storage Service (S3):** This service offers highly scalable object storage for data of all types, ranging from website content and media files to backups and archives.
  - ○ **Amazon Elastic Block Store (EBS):** This service provides block storage

volumes that can be attached to EC2 instances to provide persistent data storage for your applications.

- ○ **Amazon Relational Database Service (RDS):** This service simplifies the setup, operation, and scaling of relational databases in the cloud, supporting popular database engines such as MySQL, PostgreSQL, and Oracle.

- **Networking:**
  - ○ **Amazon Virtual Private Cloud (VPC):** This service enables you to establish a logically isolated section within the AWS cloud, allowing you to launch AWS resources in a virtual network that you define and control.
  - ○ **Amazon Route 53:** This service provides a highly available and scalable Domain Name System (DNS) web service, ensuring reliable routing of internet traffic to your applications.
  - ○ **Elastic Load Balancing:** This service distributes incoming application traffic across multiple targets, such as EC2 instances, containers, and IP

addresses, enhancing availability and fault tolerance.

- **Databases:**
  - **Amazon DynamoDB:** This service offers a fully managed, serverless, key-value NoSQL database that delivers exceptional scalability and performance.
  - **Amazon Redshift:** This service provides a fast, fully managed, petabyte-scale data warehouse service designed for high-performance analytics.
  - **Amazon Aurora:** This service offers a MySQL and PostgreSQL-compatible relational database that delivers high availability and scalability.
- **Security:**
  - **AWS Identity and Access Management (IAM):** This service enables you to manage access to AWS services and resources securely, ensuring that only authorized users and applications can interact with your cloud environment.
  - **AWS Key Management Service (KMS):** This service provides

encryption key management for your data, enabling you to protect sensitive information with encryption.

○ **AWS Security Hub:** This service offers a centralized view of your security posture across your AWS accounts, helping you identify and address potential security vulnerabilities.

- **Management Tools:**

○ **AWS CloudFormation:** This service provides a declarative way to describe and provision all the infrastructure resources in your cloud environment, enabling you to automate infrastructure deployments.

○ **AWS CloudWatch:** This service enables you to monitor your AWS resources and applications, collect and track metrics, and set alarms to notify you of potential issues.

○ **AWS CloudTrail:** This service records AWS API calls for your account and delivers log files to you, providing an audit trail of activity in your cloud environment.

Why Choose AWS?

AWS is a compelling choice for a wide range of use cases and organizations, including:

- **Startups:** AWS offers a free tier for new users, enabling startups to experiment with cloud services and gain valuable experience without incurring costs.
- **Enterprises:** AWS provides the scalability, reliability, and security that enterprises require to run mission-critical applications and support their business operations.
- **Government agencies:** AWS offers government-specific services and compliance certifications to meet the unique needs and regulatory requirements of public sector organizations.
- **Developers:** AWS provides a rich set of developer tools and services to support agile development methodologies and foster innovation.

Getting Started with AWS:

To embark on your AWS journey, you can create an AWS account and explore the free tier offerings. AWS provides comprehensive documentation, tutorials, and support resources to facilitate your learning and enable you to effectively utilize its services.

In conclusion, AWS is a powerful and versatile cloud platform that can empower your organization to innovate, grow, and achieve its business objectives. Its comprehensive suite of services, global reach, and unwavering commitment to innovation make it a leading choice for businesses of all sizes.

Azure: Microsoft Azure

Microsoft Azure, commonly known as Azure, is a robust and comprehensive cloud computing platform developed by Microsoft. Launched in 2010, Azure has rapidly grown to become a strong contender in the cloud market, offering a wide array of services that cater to diverse needs, from basic computing and storage to advanced analytics, artificial intelligence, and Internet of Things (IoT) solutions.

Key Strengths of Azure:

- **Strong Enterprise Focus:** With its deep roots in the enterprise software world, Azure has a strong focus on meeting the needs of businesses, offering seamless integration with existing Microsoft technologies and a robust set of enterprise-grade services.

- **Hybrid Cloud Capabilities:** Azure excels in hybrid cloud solutions, allowing you to seamlessly connect your on-premises infrastructure with the cloud, enabling a gradual transition and flexible deployment options.
- **Developer-Friendly:** Azure provides a rich set of developer tools and services, including support for various programming languages, frameworks, and DevOps tools, making it a preferred choice for developers.
- **Global Scale and Reliability:** Azure boasts a vast global infrastructure with data centers in numerous regions, ensuring high availability, low latency, and disaster recovery capabilities.
- **Innovation:** Microsoft is committed to innovation in the cloud, continually investing in new technologies and services, such as AI, ML, and serverless computing, to empower its customers.
- **Security and Compliance:** Azure prioritizes security and compliance, adhering to various industry standards and regulations, including ISO 27001, SOC 2, and HIPAA, to ensure the safety and privacy of your data.

Core Azure Services:

Let's explore some of the core Azure services that form the backbone of its cloud platform:

- **Compute:**
  - **Azure Virtual Machines:** Offers a wide range of virtual machines with various operating systems, sizes, and configurations to meet your compute needs.
  - **Azure Functions:** Enables serverless computing, allowing you to run code without managing servers.
  - **Azure Kubernetes Service (AKS):** Provides a managed Kubernetes service for deploying and managing containerized applications.
- **Storage:**
  - **Azure Blob Storage:** Offers scalable object storage for unstructured data like documents, media files, and backups.
  - **Azure Disk Storage:** Provides persistent disk storage for virtual machines.
  - **Azure Files:** Offers fully managed file shares in the cloud that can be accessed from anywhere.
- **Networking:**

- o **Azure Virtual Network:** Enables you to create isolated network environments in the cloud.
- o **Azure Load Balancer:** Distributes traffic across multiple instances of your application for high availability and scalability.
- o **Azure Application Gateway:** Provides a web application firewall (WAF) to protect your applications from web vulnerabilities.
- **Databases:**
  - o **Azure SQL Database:** Offers a fully managed relational database service for SQL Server workloads.
  - o **Azure Cosmos DB:** Provides a globally distributed, multi-model database service for NoSQL workloads.
  - o **Azure Database for MySQL and PostgreSQL:** Offers fully managed database services for MySQL and PostgreSQL.
- **Security:**
  - o **Azure Active Directory:** Provides identity and access management services for your cloud resources.

- o **Azure Security Center:** Offers a unified security management system for your Azure resources.
- o **Azure Key Vault:** Provides secure storage for secrets, such as passwords, certificates, and API keys.
- **Management Tools:**
  - o **Azure Resource Manager:** Enables you to deploy and manage your Azure resources in a declarative manner.
  - o **Azure Monitor:** Provides comprehensive monitoring for your Azure resources and applications.
  - o **Azure DevOps:** Offers a set of DevOps services for building, testing, and deploying applications.

Why Choose Azure?

Azure is a compelling choice for various organizations and use cases, including:

- **Enterprises with Microsoft Investments:** Azure seamlessly integrates with existing Microsoft technologies, making it a natural choice for organizations already using Microsoft products.
- **Hybrid Cloud Deployments:** Azure's strong hybrid cloud capabilities enable

organizations to gradually transition to the cloud while maintaining their on-premises infrastructure.

- **.NET Developers:** Azure provides excellent support for .NET development, making it a preferred platform for .NET applications.
- **Data-Driven Organizations:** Azure offers a comprehensive suite of data services, including data warehousing, analytics, and machine learning, to empower data-driven decision-making.

Getting Started with Azure:

To get started with Azure, you can create a free Azure account and explore the free services and trial offers. Microsoft provides extensive documentation, tutorials, and support resources to help you learn and use Azure effectively.

In conclusion, Azure is a powerful and versatile cloud platform that offers a wide range of services to meet the needs of businesses of all sizes. Its strong enterprise focus, hybrid cloud capabilities, and commitment to innovation make it a compelling choice for organizations seeking to leverage the power of the cloud.

GCP: Google Cloud Platform

Google Cloud Platform (GCP) is a comprehensive suite of cloud computing services offered by Google. Launched in 2008, GCP has emerged as a major player in the cloud arena, providing a wide range of services, from computing and storage to data analytics, artificial intelligence, and machine learning. GCP leverages Google's expertise in data management, networking, and innovation to deliver powerful and scalable solutions for businesses of all sizes.

Key Strengths of GCP:

- **Data Analytics and Machine Learning:** GCP excels in data analytics and machine learning, offering a rich set of tools and services, such as BigQuery, Cloud AI Platform, and TensorFlow, that empower organizations to extract insights from their data and build intelligent applications.
- **Kubernetes Expertise:** Google is the creator of Kubernetes, the leading open-source container orchestration system. GCP's managed Kubernetes service, Google Kubernetes Engine (GKE), is widely regarded as the industry's best-of-breed Kubernetes offering.

- **Open Source Commitment:** GCP embraces open source technologies, contributing to and supporting various open source projects, making it a preferred choice for developers and organizations that value open standards.
- **Global Network Infrastructure:** GCP leverages Google's global network infrastructure, one of the largest and most advanced in the world, to deliver high performance, low latency, and global reach for its services.
- **Competitive Pricing:** GCP offers competitive pricing models, including sustained use discounts and flexible payment options, to help you optimize your cloud spending.
- **Security and Compliance:** GCP prioritizes security and compliance, adhering to various industry standards and regulations, including ISO 27001, SOC 2, and HIPAA, to ensure the safety and privacy of your data.

Core GCP Services:

Let's explore some of the core GCP services that form the foundation of its cloud platform:

- **Compute:**

- **Google Compute Engine:** Provides virtual machines with a variety of machine types, operating systems, and configurations to meet your compute needs.
- **Google App Engine:** Offers a serverless platform for building and deploying web applications and APIs.
- **Google Kubernetes Engine (GKE):** Provides a managed Kubernetes service for deploying and managing containerized applications.

- **Storage:**
  - **Google Cloud Storage:** Offers scalable object storage for data of all types, from backups and archives to media files and website content.
  - **Google Cloud SQL:** Provides fully managed relational databases for MySQL, PostgreSQL, and SQL Server.
  - **Google Cloud Spanner:** Offers a globally distributed, scalable, and strongly consistent database service.

- **Networking:**
  - **Google Virtual Private Cloud (VPC):** Enables you to create isolated network environments in the cloud.

- o **Google Cloud Load Balancing:** Distributes traffic across multiple instances of your application for high availability and scalability.
- o **Google Cloud DNS:** Provides a reliable and scalable DNS service for your applications.
- **Databases:**
  - o **Google Cloud Datastore:** Offers a highly scalable NoSQL document database for web and mobile applications.
  - o **Google BigQuery:** Provides a serverless, highly scalable, and cost-effective multi-cloud data warehouse for analytics.
  - o **Google Cloud Firestore:** Offers a flexible NoSQL document database for mobile, web, and server development.
- **Big Data and Analytics:**
  - o **Google Cloud Dataproc:** Provides a managed Hadoop and Spark service for big data processing.
  - o **Google Cloud Dataflow:** Offers a serverless data processing service for batch and stream data.

- **Google Cloud Pub/Sub:** Provides a real-time messaging service for distributing events and data.
- **Security:**
  - **Google Cloud Identity and Access Management (IAM):** Enables you to manage access to GCP resources securely.
  - **Google Cloud Key Management Service (KMS):** Provides encryption key management for your data.
  - **Google Cloud Security Command Center:** Offers a security and data risk platform for your GCP resources.
- **Management Tools:**
  - **Google Cloud Console:** Provides a web-based interface for managing your GCP resources.
  - **Google Cloud SDK:** Offers command-line tools for interacting with GCP services.
  - **Google Cloud Deployment Manager:** Enables you to automate the deployment and management of your GCP resources.

Why Choose GCP?

GCP is a compelling choice for various organizations and use cases, including:

- **Data-Driven Organizations:** GCP's strengths in data analytics and machine learning make it a preferred choice for organizations seeking to extract insights from their data and build intelligent applications.
- **Kubernetes Users:** GCP's expertise in Kubernetes and its managed Kubernetes service, GKE, make it an ideal platform for deploying and managing containerized applications.
- **Open Source Advocates:** GCP's commitment to open source technologies and its contributions to various open source projects make it a preferred choice for developers and organizations that value open standards.
- **Startups and Small Businesses:** GCP offers a free tier for new users and competitive pricing models, making it an attractive option for startups and small businesses.

Getting Started with GCP:

To get started with GCP, you can create a free GCP account and explore the free tier offerings. Google provides extensive documentation, tutorials, and support resources to help you learn and use GCP effectively.

In conclusion, GCP is a powerful and innovative cloud platform that offers a wide range of services to meet the needs of businesses of all sizes. Its strengths in data analytics, machine learning, Kubernetes, and open source technologies make it a compelling choice for organizations seeking to leverage the power of the cloud.

Part II: Core Cloud Services

Chapter 4: Compute Services

Virtual Machines (VMs)

Imagine having the ability to run a complete computer system within your own computer. This, essentially, is the concept of a virtual machine (VM). A VM is a software-based emulation of a physical computer, capable of running its own operating system and applications independently, completely isolated from the underlying hardware. It's akin to having multiple, self-contained computers operating on a single physical machine.

The Mechanics of Virtualization:

VMs are made possible through a technology called **virtualization**. A specialized software layer, known as a **hypervisor**, acts as an intermediary between the physical hardware and the VMs. The hypervisor is responsible for managing and allocating essential resources such as CPU power, memory, and storage to each individual VM. This ingenious mechanism allows multiple VMs to share the same physical hardware resources while remaining completely isolated from one another, preventing interference and conflicts.

Dissecting a VM:

- **Guest OS:** This refers to the operating system that runs within the VM environment. Importantly, the guest OS can be different from the host OS, providing flexibility in software choices.
- **Virtual Hardware:** VMs utilize emulated hardware components, including virtual CPUs, memory, network interfaces, and storage, to create a complete and functional computing environment.
- **Hypervisor:** As mentioned earlier, the hypervisor is the software layer that orchestrates the allocation of resources to the VMs, ensuring efficient operation and isolation.
- **Host OS:** This is the operating system running on the physical machine that hosts the VMs.

Advantages of Utilizing VMs:

- **Enhanced Resource Efficiency:** VMs enable the consolidation of multiple physical servers onto a single host machine, maximizing resource utilization and significantly reducing hardware costs.
- **Robust Isolation:** VMs provide strong isolation between applications and

workloads, enhancing security by preventing interference and containing potential issues.

- **Unparalleled Flexibility:** VMs allow you to run different operating systems and applications on the same physical hardware, providing flexibility and adaptability to meet diverse needs.
- **Effortless Scalability:** VMs can be easily scaled up or down to accommodate changing demands, ensuring optimal performance and resource allocation.
- **Seamless Portability:** VMs can be readily moved between different physical hosts or cloud providers, facilitating migration and disaster recovery efforts.
- **Significant Cost Savings:** By reducing the need for physical hardware, VMs contribute to cost savings in terms of hardware acquisition, energy consumption, and administrative overhead.

Applications of VMs in the Cloud:

- **Web Hosting:** VMs provide a reliable and scalable platform for hosting websites and web applications in the cloud.
- **Application Development and Testing:** VMs offer isolated environments for

developing and testing applications, ensuring consistency and preventing conflicts.

- **Data Analytics and Machine Learning:** Powerful VMs can handle data-intensive workloads and execute complex machine learning models efficiently.
- **Disaster Recovery:** VMs play a crucial role in disaster recovery strategies by replicating critical systems and data to the cloud, ensuring business continuity.
- **Legacy Application Support:** VMs can extend the lifespan of legacy applications by providing a compatible environment for them to run in the cloud.

VMs in the Cloud Computing Landscape:

Cloud providers offer a diverse range of VM instances with varying configurations to cater to a wide array of needs. You can select the appropriate number of virtual CPUs (vCPUs), amount of memory, storage capacity, and networking options based on the specific requirements of your applications.

Leading Cloud VM Services:

- **AWS EC2 (Amazon Elastic Compute Cloud):** AWS provides a comprehensive selection of VM instances with diverse configurations and flexible pricing options to suit various workloads and budgets.

- **Azure Virtual Machines:** Azure offers VMs running both Windows and Linux operating systems, seamlessly integrated with other Azure services for a cohesive cloud experience.
- **Google Compute Engine:** Google's Compute Engine delivers VMs with customizable machine types and high-performance networking capabilities, ensuring optimal performance for demanding applications.

Managing VMs in the Cloud:

Cloud providers offer a suite of tools and services to simplify the management of your VMs, including:

- **VM Creation and Configuration:** User-friendly interfaces and APIs enable easy creation and configuration of VMs, streamlining deployment processes.
- **VM Monitoring and Management:** Comprehensive monitoring tools provide insights into VM performance, resource utilization, and overall health, facilitating proactive management.

- **VM Scaling:** Cloud platforms allow you to scale your VMs up or down dynamically based on demand, ensuring optimal resource allocation and cost efficiency.
- **VM Security:** Robust security measures, including firewalls, access control, and security groups, help protect your VMs from unauthorized access and threats.

Selecting the Optimal VM:

Choosing the right VM requires careful consideration of several factors:

- **Workload Requirements:** Assess your application's needs in terms of CPU, memory, storage, and network bandwidth to select a VM with appropriate resources.
- **Operating System:** Choose the operating system that best suits your application's requirements and your team's expertise.
- **Pricing:** Evaluate different pricing models and select the most cost-effective option based on your usage patterns and budget constraints.
- **Performance:** Consider factors such as network performance and storage I/O to ensure your VM delivers the required performance for your applications.

- **Security:** Prioritize security by selecting a VM that meets your security requirements and complies with relevant industry standards and regulations.

By grasping the capabilities and advantages of virtual machines, you can effectively leverage them to build, deploy, and manage scalable and reliable applications in the cloud.

Containers (Docker, Kubernetes)

While virtual machines revolutionized how we utilize hardware, containers take application deployment and management to the next level. Containers offer a lightweight and portable approach to packaging and running applications, providing greater efficiency and flexibility compared to traditional VMs.

What are Containers?

A container is a standardized, executable package of software that includes everything needed to run an application: code, runtime, system tools, system libraries, and settings.[1] Unlike VMs, containers share the host operating system kernel but maintain isolated user spaces. This makes them significantly smaller and more efficient than VMs, as they don't need to include a full operating system for each application.

Benefits of Containers:

- **Lightweight:** Containers are much smaller than VMs, requiring less storage space and resources.
- **Portability:** Containers can run on any platform that supports the container runtime, ensuring consistency across different environments.
- **Efficiency:** Containers share the host OS kernel, reducing overhead and improving resource utilization.
- **Speed:** Containers start and stop much faster than VMs, enabling rapid deployment and scaling.
- **Consistency:** Containers package all dependencies, ensuring consistent behavior across different environments.
- **Microservices:** Containers are ideal for building and deploying microservices-based architectures.

Docker: The Containerization Platform

Docker is the most popular containerization platform, providing tools and technologies for building, shipping, and running containers.

Key Docker Components:

- **Docker Engine:** The core runtime environment for building and running containers.
- **Docker Images:** Read-only templates used to create containers.
- **Docker Hub:** A public registry for storing and sharing Docker images.
- **Docker Compose:** A tool for defining and managing multi-container applications.

Kubernetes: The Container Orchestrator

As you deploy more containers, managing them individually becomes challenging. This is where Kubernetes comes in. Kubernetes is an open-source system for automating the deployment, scaling, and management of containerized applications.

Key[2] Kubernetes Features:

- **Automated Deployment:** Kubernetes automates the deployment and scaling of containers across a cluster of machines.

- **Self-Healing:** Kubernetes monitors the health of containers and automatically restarts or replaces failed containers.
- **Load Balancing:** Kubernetes distributes traffic across multiple containers to ensure high availability.
- **Service Discovery:** Kubernetes provides a mechanism for containers to discover and communicate with each other.
- **Storage Orchestration:** Kubernetes mounts storage volumes to containers, providing persistent storage.
- **Secrets Management:** Kubernetes securely stores and manages sensitive information like passwords and API keys.

Why Use Containers in Cloud Computing?

- **Microservices:** Containers are ideal for building and deploying microservices-based architectures, enabling you to break down your applications into smaller, independent services.
- **Scalability:** Containers can be easily scaled up or down to meet changing demands, providing flexibility and efficiency.
- **Portability:** Containers can be deployed on any cloud platform that supports Docker and

Kubernetes, providing flexibility and avoiding vendor lock-in.

- **DevOps:** Containers facilitate DevOps practices by enabling continuous integration and continuous delivery (CI/CD).

Container Services in the Cloud:

- **AWS ECS (Elastic Container Service) and EKS (Elastic Kubernetes Service):** AWS offers both a managed container service (ECS) and a managed Kubernetes service (EKS).
- **Azure Kubernetes Service (AKS):** Azure provides a managed Kubernetes service for deploying and managing containerized applications.
- **Google Kubernetes Engine (GKE):** Google, the creator of Kubernetes, offers a managed Kubernetes service with advanced features and integrations.

Conclusion:

Containers are transforming how applications are built, deployed, and managed in the cloud. By leveraging containerization technologies like Docker and Kubernetes, you can achieve greater efficiency, scalability, and portability for your cloud applications.

Serverless Computing (AWS Lambda, Azure Functions)

Imagine running your code without worrying about servers, operating systems, or infrastructure management. This is the promise of serverless computing, a cloud execution model where the cloud provider dynamically manages the allocation of machine resources. You simply write and upload your code, and the cloud provider takes care of everything else, from scaling to security.

What is Serverless Computing?

Serverless computing, despite its name, doesn't mean there are no servers involved. It simply means that you, as the developer, don't need to manage them. The cloud provider handles all the underlying infrastructure, allowing you to focus solely on writing and deploying your code.

Key Characteristics of Serverless Computing:

- **No Server Management:** You don't need to provision, configure, or maintain servers.
- **Automatic Scaling:** The cloud provider automatically scales your application up or down based on demand.

- **Pay-as-you-go Pricing:** You only pay for the compute time your code consumes.
- **Event-Driven Architecture:** Serverless functions are typically triggered by events, such as HTTP requests, database changes, or messages from a queue.
- **Microservices:** Serverless computing is well-suited for building and deploying microservices.

Benefits of Serverless Computing:

- **Reduced Operational Overhead:** No need to manage servers or operating systems, freeing up your team to focus on development.
- **Cost Efficiency:** Pay only for the compute time your code consumes, eliminating the cost of idle servers.
- **Scalability:** Automatic scaling ensures your application can handle spikes in traffic without manual intervention.
- **Faster Time to Market:** Focus on writing code and deploying it quickly, without infrastructure setup delays.
- **Increased Agility:** Easily adapt to changing requirements and deploy new features rapidly.

Use Cases for Serverless Computing:

- **Web Applications:** Build and deploy web applications and APIs.
- **Data Processing:** Process data in real-time or in batch mode.
- **Backend Services:** Create backend services for mobile and web applications.
- **Chatbots and Virtual Assistants:** Develop conversational interfaces and chatbots.
- **IoT Applications:** Process data from IoT devices and trigger actions based on events.

AWS Lambda:

AWS Lambda is a leading serverless compute service that lets you run code without provisioning or managing servers. You can upload your code as a ZIP file or container image, and Lambda automatically runs it in response to events.

Key Features of AWS Lambda:

- **Support for Multiple Languages:** Run code written in languages like Python, Node.js, Java, Go, Ruby, and C#.
- **Integration with Other AWS Services:** Seamlessly integrate with other AWS services like S3, DynamoDB, API Gateway, and Kinesis.

- **Concurrency Control:** Control the number of concurrent executions to manage resource usage and costs.
- **Monitoring and Logging:** Monitor function performance and troubleshoot issues with CloudWatch.

Azure Functions:

Azure Functions is Microsoft's serverless compute service that enables you to run event-driven code without managing infrastructure. You can write functions[1] in various languages and deploy them to Azure.

Key Features of Azure Functions:

- **Variety of Triggers:** Trigger functions based on events like HTTP requests, timer schedules, queue messages, and blob storage changes.
- **Integration with Azure Services:** Integrate with other Azure services like Cosmos DB, Event Hubs, and Service Bus.
- **Durable Functions:** Build stateful functions that can handle long-running operations.
- **Monitoring and Logging:** Monitor function performance and troubleshoot issues with Azure Monitor.

Choosing a Serverless Platform:

When choosing a serverless platform, consider factors like:

- **Supported Languages:** Ensure the platform supports your preferred programming language.
- **Integrations:** Choose a platform that integrates well with other cloud services you use.
- **Pricing:** Compare pricing models and choose the most cost-effective option for your needs.
- **Features:** Consider features like concurrency control, monitoring, and logging.

Conclusion:

Serverless computing is revolutionizing how applications are built and deployed in the cloud. By leveraging serverless platforms like AWS Lambda and Azure Functions, you can reduce operational overhead, optimize costs, and increase agility for your cloud applications.

Chapter 5: Storage Services

Object Storage (S3, Azure Blob Storage, Google Cloud Storage)

In the world of cloud computing, storing data efficiently, securely, and cost-effectively is paramount. Object storage has emerged as a leading solution for managing vast amounts of unstructured data, such as images, videos, documents, and log files. Unlike traditional file storage systems, object storage treats data as discrete units, or "objects," each with its own unique identifier and metadata. This approach offers significant advantages in terms of scalability, flexibility, and cost-efficiency.

What is Object Storage?

Object storage is a method of storing data in a hierarchical structure where files are broken down into units called "objects" and placed in a flat address space called a "bucket" or "container." Each object comprises the data itself, metadata describing the data, and a unique identifier that allows for retrieval.

Key Characteristics of Object Storage:

- **Scalability:** Object storage is designed to scale horizontally, allowing you to store virtually unlimited amounts of data.
- **Durability and Availability:** Data is typically replicated across multiple devices and locations, ensuring high durability and availability.
- **Flexibility:** Object storage can handle various data types, from small text files to large multimedia files.
- **Metadata:** Each object includes metadata, providing valuable information about the data and enabling efficient search and retrieval.
- **Cost-Efficiency:** Object storage typically offers cost-effective storage options, especially for infrequently accessed data.

Benefits of Object Storage:

- **Massive Scalability:** Store petabytes or even exabytes of data without performance degradation.
- **High Durability and Availability:** Data is protected from loss or downtime due to replication and redundancy.
- **Cost-Effectiveness:** Optimize storage costs by selecting different storage classes based on data access patterns.

- **Flexibility:** Store diverse data types, including images, videos, backups, and log files.
- **Enhanced Security:** Access control mechanisms and encryption protect data from unauthorized access.

Leading Cloud Object Storage Services:

- **Amazon S3 (Simple Storage Service):** A highly scalable, reliable, and cost-effective object storage service offered by AWS. S3 provides a wide range of storage classes, including Standard, Intelligent-Tiering, Glacier, and Deep Archive, to optimize costs based on access frequency.
- **Azure Blob Storage:** Azure's object storage service for storing massive amounts of unstructured data. Blob storage offers different access tiers, including Hot, Cool, and Archive, to balance cost and performance.
- **Google Cloud Storage:** GCP's highly scalable and durable object storage service. Cloud Storage offers various storage classes, including Standard, Nearline, Coldline, and Archive, to meet different data access needs.

Common Features of Cloud Object Storage:

- **Buckets/Containers:** Data is organized into buckets (S3, Google Cloud Storage) or containers (Azure Blob Storage).
- **Storage Classes:** Choose from different storage classes based on access frequency and cost considerations.
- **Versioning:** Maintain multiple versions of objects, enabling data recovery and rollback.
- **Lifecycle Management:** Automate data movement between storage classes based on predefined rules.
- **Encryption:** Protect data at rest and in transit with encryption.
- **Access Control:** Control access to data with granular permissions.

Use Cases for Object Storage:

- **Data Archiving and Backup:** Store infrequently accessed data, backups, and archives cost-effectively.
- **Media Storage and Delivery:** Store and deliver images, videos, and other media content.
- **Data Lakes:** Build data lakes for big data analytics and machine learning.
- **Website Hosting:** Host static websites and web applications.

- **Software Distribution:** Distribute software packages and updates.

Choosing the Right Object Storage Service:

When selecting an object storage service, consider factors like:

- **Storage Capacity and Scalability:** Ensure the service can handle your current and future storage needs.
- **Performance:** Evaluate performance based on data access patterns and latency requirements.
- **Storage Classes and Pricing:** Choose storage classes and pricing models that align with your budget and access patterns.
- **Data Availability and Durability:** Ensure the service meets your requirements for data availability and durability.
- **Security and Compliance:** Select a service that meets your security and compliance requirements.
- **Integration with Other Services:** Choose a service that integrates well with other cloud services you use.

Conclusion:

Object storage is a powerful and versatile solution for managing vast amounts of unstructured data in the cloud. By leveraging cloud object storage services like Amazon S3, Azure Blob Storage, and Google Cloud Storage, you can achieve scalability, cost-efficiency, and high availability for your data storage needs.

Databases (Relational, NoSQL)

Databases are the bedrock of modern applications, providing a structured and organized way to store, manage, and retrieve data. In the cloud computing landscape, databases play a crucial role in powering everything from web applications and mobile apps to data analytics and machine learning. Cloud providers offer a wide variety of database services, catering to different data models, scalability needs, and performance requirements.

Relational Databases:

Relational databases have been the cornerstone of data management for decades. They organize data into tables with rows and columns, establishing relationships between different tables through keys. This structured approach ensures data integrity and consistency, making relational databases ideal for applications that require ACID properties (Atomicity, Consistency, Isolation, Durability).

Key Characteristics of Relational Databases:

- **Structured Data:** Data is organized into tables with predefined schemas.
- **Relationships:** Tables are related to each other through keys, enabling efficient querying and data retrieval.
- **SQL:** Structured Query Language (SQL) is used to interact with the database, providing a powerful and standardized way to query, update, and manage data.
- **ACID Properties:** Relational databases ensure data integrity and consistency through ACID properties.
- **Normalization:** Data is typically normalized to reduce redundancy and improve data integrity.

Popular Relational Database Management Systems (RDBMS):

- **MySQL:** An open-source relational database management system known for its ease of use and performance.

- **PostgreSQL:** A powerful open-source relational database system known for its advanced features and extensibility.
- **SQL Server:** Microsoft's relational database management system, offering enterprise-grade features and scalability.
- **Oracle Database:** A robust and scalable relational database system commonly used in enterprise environments.

NoSQL Databases:

NoSQL databases have emerged as a popular alternative to relational databases, particularly for handling large volumes of unstructured or semi-structured data. NoSQL databases offer greater flexibility and scalability than relational databases, making them well-suited for cloud-native applications and big data workloads.

Key Characteristics of NoSQL Databases:

- **Flexible Schema:** NoSQL databases allow for flexible schemas, accommodating data that doesn't fit neatly into tables.
- **Scalability:** NoSQL databases are designed to scale horizontally, handling massive amounts of data and traffic.

- **Variety of Data Models:** NoSQL databases support various data models, including document, key-value, graph, and column-family.
- **High Availability:** NoSQL databases often offer high availability and fault tolerance through data replication and distribution.
- **Eventual Consistency:** Some NoSQL databases prioritize availability over strong consistency, offering eventual consistency where data is eventually consistent across all replicas.

Types of NoSQL Databases:

- **Document Databases:** Store data in JSON-like documents, offering flexibility and ease of use. (e.g., MongoDB, Couchbase)
- **Key-Value Stores:** Store data as key-value pairs, providing high performance and scalability for simple data structures. (e.g., Redis, Memcached)
- **Graph Databases:** Store data as nodes and relationships, ideal for social networks, recommendation engines, and knowledge graphs. (e.g., Neo4j, Amazon Neptune)
- **Column-Family Stores:** Store data in columns instead of rows, providing high

performance for read-heavy workloads. (e.g., Cassandra, HBase)

Choosing the Right Database:

Selecting the appropriate database for your application depends on several factors:

- **Data Model:** Choose a database that aligns with the structure and type of data you need to store.
- **Scalability:** Consider the scalability requirements of your application and choose a database that can handle your anticipated growth.
- **Performance:** Evaluate the performance characteristics of the database, considering factors like read/write speeds, latency, and throughput.
- **Consistency:** Determine the level of data consistency required for your application and choose a database that meets those needs.
- **Cost:** Compare the pricing models of different database services and choose the most cost-effective option for your budget.

Cloud Database Services:

Cloud providers offer a wide range of managed database services, simplifying database administration and maintenance:

- **AWS:** Amazon RDS (Relational Database Service), Amazon DynamoDB, Amazon Aurora, Amazon Redshift
- **Azure:** Azure SQL Database, Azure Cosmos DB, Azure Database for MySQL, Azure Database for PostgreSQL
- **GCP:** Google Cloud SQL, Google Cloud Spanner, Google Cloud Datastore, Google BigQuery

Conclusion:

Databases are essential components of cloud applications, providing a structured and organized way to store, manage, and retrieve data. By understanding the different types of databases, their characteristics, and the cloud database services available, you can choose the right database for your application and leverage the power of the cloud for your data management needs.

Data Warehousing

5.3 Data Warehousing

While databases excel at handling transactional data and supporting day-to-day operations, data warehouses are designed for a different purpose: **analytical processing**. Data warehouses are centralized repositories that consolidate data from various sources, transforming it into a format optimized for analysis, reporting, and business intelligence. They provide a historical perspective on your data, enabling you to identify trends, patterns, and insights that can drive informed decision-making.

What is a Data Warehouse?

A data warehouse is a specialized database designed for analytical processing. It stores large volumes of historical data extracted from various sources, such as transactional databases, operational systems, and external data feeds. This data is cleaned, transformed, and organized into a structure that facilitates efficient querying and analysis.

Key Characteristics of a Data Warehouse:

- **Subject-Oriented:** Data is organized around specific subjects or business areas, such as sales, marketing, or finance.

- **Integrated:** Data from different sources is consolidated and standardized to ensure consistency and accuracy.
- **Time-Variant:** Data is stored with timestamps, providing a historical perspective and enabling trend analysis.
- **Non-Volatile:** Data is not updated or deleted once it's loaded into the data warehouse, ensuring a consistent historical record.
- **Optimized for Read Operations:** Data warehouses are designed for analytical queries, prioritizing read performance over write performance.

Benefits of Data Warehousing:

- **Improved Business Intelligence:** Data warehouses provide a comprehensive view of your data, enabling you to gain deeper insights into your business and make informed decisions.
- **Enhanced Data Analysis:** Data warehouses facilitate complex analytical queries, allowing you to identify trends, patterns, and anomalies in your data.
- **Increased Efficiency:** Data warehouses streamline data access and analysis, reducing the time and effort required to extract valuable insights.

- **Better Decision-Making:** Data warehouses empower you to make data-driven decisions based on historical trends and patterns.
- **Improved Data Quality:** Data cleansing and transformation processes in data warehousing improve data quality and consistency.

Building a Data Warehouse:

Building a data warehouse involves several key steps:

1. **Data Extraction:** Extract data from various sources, such as transactional databases, operational systems, and external data feeds.
2. **Data Cleaning and Transformation:** Cleanse and transform the extracted data to ensure consistency, accuracy, and compatibility.
3. **Data Loading:** Load the transformed data into the data warehouse.
4. **Data Modeling:** Design the structure of the data warehouse, organizing data into tables and relationships that facilitate analysis.
5. **Data Analysis and Reporting:** Use analytical tools and techniques to query and

analyze the data, generating reports and visualizations.

Data Warehouse Architectures:

- **Traditional Data Warehouse:** A centralized repository that stores data from various sources in a relational database.
- **Data Mart:** A smaller, focused data warehouse that serves a specific department or business unit.
- **Cloud Data Warehouse:** A data warehouse hosted in the cloud, offering scalability, flexibility, and cost-efficiency.

Cloud Data Warehouse Services:

Cloud providers offer managed data warehouse services that simplify data warehousing and reduce operational overhead:

- **AWS Redshift:** A fast, scalable, and fully managed cloud data warehouse service.
- **Azure Synapse Analytics:** A limitless analytics service that brings together data warehousing, big data analytics, and data integration.
- **Google BigQuery:** A serverless, highly scalable, and cost-effective multi-cloud data warehouse.

Choosing a Data Warehouse Solution:

When selecting a data warehouse solution, consider factors like:

- **Data Volume and Scalability:** Choose a solution that can handle your current and future data volume and scalability needs.

- **Performance:** Evaluate the performance characteristics of the data warehouse, considering factors like query speed and concurrency.

- **Cost:** Compare the pricing models of different data warehouse services and choose the most cost-effective option for your budget.

- **Integration with Other Services:** Choose a solution that integrates well with other cloud services you use, such as data integration tools and analytics platforms.

- **Security and Compliance:** Select a solution that meets your security and compliance requirements.

Conclusion:

Data warehousing is a crucial component of business intelligence and data analytics, providing a historical perspective on your data and enabling you to extract valuable insights. By leveraging cloud data warehouse services, you can simplify data warehousing, reduce operational overhead, and gain a competitive advantage through data-driven decision-making.

Chapter 6: Networking Fundamentals

Virtual Private Clouds (VPCs)

Imagine establishing your own exclusive enclave within the vast expanse of the internet, a secure and isolated domain where you can deploy and manage your cloud resources without interference from other users. This is the essence of a Virtual Private Cloud (VPC). A VPC is a logically isolated section of a public cloud provider's network that you control, giving you the power to define your own network configuration, including IP address ranges, subnets, route tables, and security policies.

Understanding VPCs

Think of a VPC as a virtual network carved out within the larger public cloud. It provides a private IP address space that is segregated from other VPCs and the public internet. You have complete autonomy over this virtual network, enabling you to tailor it to your specific security and networking requirements.

Defining Features of VPCs:

- **Isolation:** VPCs create a secure and isolated environment for your cloud resources, shielding them from unauthorized access and potential threats.

- **Customization:** You have granular control over your VPC's network configuration, including IP address ranges, subnets, and route tables, allowing you to tailor it to your specific needs.
- **Security:** Implement robust security measures like security groups and network access control lists (ACLs) to regulate traffic flow within your VPC and protect your resources.
- **Connectivity:** Establish connections between your VPC and your on-premises network or other VPCs to create hybrid cloud environments and extend your network reach.
- **Scalability:** VPCs are designed to scale seamlessly, accommodating your evolving needs by allowing you to add or remove resources as required.

Advantages of Employing VPCs:

- **Reinforced Security:** Isolate your cloud resources from other users and the public internet, mitigating the risk of unauthorized access and security breaches.

- **Enhanced Network Control:** Define your own network configuration, including IP address ranges, subnets, and routing policies, to align with your specific requirements.
- **Streamlined Network Management:** Manage your network resources efficiently through a centralized and organized approach.
- **Increased Agility:** Create complex network topologies and connect your VPC to your on-premises network or other VPCs to support diverse deployment scenarios.
- **Cost Optimization:** Optimize network costs by controlling network traffic flow and utilizing resources efficiently, minimizing unnecessary expenses.

Essential VPC Components:

- **IP Address Range (CIDR Block):** This defines the range of IP addresses that your VPC will utilize for its internal network.
- **Subnets:** Subnets are segments within your VPC that divide your IP address range into smaller, more manageable units, enhancing organization and security.
- **Route Tables:** Route tables determine how network traffic is directed within your VPC

and to external networks, enabling you to control traffic flow.

- **Internet Gateway:** An internet gateway facilitates communication between your VPC and the public internet, allowing your resources to access external services.
- **Virtual Private Gateway:** A virtual private gateway establishes a secure connection between your VPC and your on-premises network, enabling hybrid cloud deployments.
- **Security Groups and Network ACLs:** Security groups and network ACLs act as virtual firewalls, allowing you to define rules that control inbound and outbound traffic to your instances and subnets, bolstering security.

Practical Applications of VPCs:

- **Web Application Hosting:** Host web applications in a secure and isolated environment, protecting them from external threats and ensuring data privacy.
- **Database Deployment:** Deploy databases in a VPC with restricted access controls to enhance security and safeguard sensitive data.
- **Application Development and Testing:** Create isolated environments for

development and testing, preventing interference and ensuring consistent results.

- **Hybrid Cloud Architectures:** Connect your VPC to your on-premises network to create a hybrid cloud environment, extending your infrastructure and leveraging the benefits of both on-premises and cloud resources.
- **Microservices Deployment:** Isolate microservices within different subnets to enhance security, fault tolerance, and granular control over service interactions.

VPC Offerings from Major Cloud Providers:

- **Amazon VPC:** Amazon Web Services offers a feature-rich and highly customizable VPC service that provides extensive control over your network environment.
- **Azure Virtual Network:** Microsoft Azure's Virtual Network service seamlessly integrates with other Azure services, providing a cohesive and comprehensive cloud networking solution.
- **Google Virtual Private Cloud:** Google Cloud Platform's VPC service leverages Google's global network infrastructure, offering high performance, low latency, and global reach for your applications.

Recommended Practices for VPC Design:

- **Strategic IP Address Planning:** Carefully plan your IP address space, allocating sufficient IP addresses to accommodate your current and future needs, preventing address exhaustion and network disruptions.
- **Effective Network Segmentation:** Utilize subnets to segment your network into smaller, more manageable units, enhancing security by isolating different workloads and applications.
- **Robust Security Implementation:** Implement security groups and network ACLs to control traffic flow within your VPC and to external networks, preventing unauthorized access and protecting your resources.
- **Proactive VPC Monitoring:** Monitor network traffic, performance, and security to ensure optimal operation, identify potential issues, and maintain a secure and efficient network environment.

In Conclusion:

VPCs are a cornerstone of cloud networking, providing a secure and isolated environment for your cloud resources. By understanding the concepts and benefits of VPCs, you can effectively design and manage your cloud networks, ensuring security, flexibility, and cost optimization for your applications and workloads.

Subnets and Routing

In the realm of networking, whether traditional or in the cloud, efficient organization and traffic management are crucial. This is where subnets and routing come into play. Subnets allow you to segment your network into smaller, more manageable units, while routing ensures that network traffic flows efficiently between these subnets and to external destinations.

What are Subnets?

A subnet, short for "subnetwork," is a logical subdivision of an IP network. It essentially divides a larger network into smaller, more manageable segments. In the context of VPCs, subnets allow you to partition your virtual network into isolated sections, enhancing security, organization, and network performance.

Benefits of Using Subnets:

- **Enhanced Security:** Isolate different applications and workloads within separate subnets, limiting the impact of security breaches and containing potential issues.

- **Improved Network Performance:** Reduce network congestion and improve performance by segmenting traffic within smaller subnets.
- **Efficient IP Address Allocation:** Allocate IP addresses more efficiently by assigning specific address ranges to different subnets.
- **Simplified Network Management:** Manage network resources more effectively by organizing them into logical groupings.
- **Geographic Isolation:** Create subnets in different Availability Zones (AZs) to ensure high availability and fault tolerance.

Subnet Mask and CIDR Notation:

Subnets are defined using a subnet mask, which determines the number of IP addresses within the subnet. CIDR (Classless Inter-Domain Routing) notation is commonly used to represent subnet masks. For example, a CIDR block of `10.0.0.0/24` represents a subnet with 256 IP addresses.

Types of Subnets in a VPC:

- **Public Subnets:** Subnets that have a route to an internet gateway, allowing resources within them to communicate with the internet.

- **Private Subnets:** Subnets that do not have a route to an internet gateway, isolating resources within them from the public internet.
- **Database Subnets:** Subnets specifically designed for hosting database instances, often with stricter security controls.

What is Routing?

Routing is the process of directing network traffic from its source to its destination. In the context of VPCs, routing determines how traffic flows between subnets within your VPC and to external networks, such as the internet or your on-premises network.

Route Tables:

Route tables are used to define routing rules within a VPC. Each subnet within your VPC is associated with a route table. Route tables contain a set of rules that specify how traffic originating from the subnet should be directed.

Types of Routes:

- **Local Route:** A default route that directs traffic within the same VPC.

- **Internet Gateway Route:** A route that directs traffic to the internet gateway for communication with the public internet.
- **Virtual Private Gateway Route:** A route that directs traffic to the virtual private gateway for communication with your on-premises network.
- **NAT Gateway Route:** A route that directs traffic to a NAT gateway to enable instances in a private subnet to access the internet.

Importance of Routing in VPCs:

- **Network Connectivity:** Routing ensures that your resources can communicate with each other and with external networks.
- **Security:** Control traffic flow and restrict access to specific resources or subnets.
- **High Availability:** Route traffic to different Availability Zones to ensure high availability and fault tolerance.
- **Network Performance:** Optimize network performance by directing traffic efficiently.

Working with Subnets and Routing in the Cloud:

Cloud providers offer tools and services to manage subnets and routing within your VPCs:

- **Subnet Creation and Management:** Create, modify, and delete subnets within your VPC.
- **Route Table Management:** Create and manage route tables, adding and removing routes as needed.
- **Network Monitoring:** Monitor network traffic flow and performance to identify and resolve issues.

Best Practices for Subnets and Routing:

- **Plan your subnet structure carefully:** Consider your security and network performance requirements when designing your subnets.
- **Use meaningful names for your subnets:** Use descriptive names that reflect the purpose of each subnet.
- **Document your routing rules:** Maintain clear documentation of your routing rules to facilitate troubleshooting and network management.
- **Monitor your network traffic:** Monitor network traffic flow and performance to identify and address potential issues.

Conclusion:

Subnets and routing are essential components of VPC networking, enabling you to segment your network, control traffic flow, and optimize network performance. By understanding these concepts and utilizing the tools provided by cloud providers, you can effectively manage your cloud networks and ensure secure and efficient communication between your resources.

Security Groups and Firewalls

In the interconnected world of cloud computing, security is paramount. Protecting your valuable data and applications from unauthorized access and malicious attacks is crucial for maintaining the integrity and availability of your cloud infrastructure. Security groups and firewalls are essential tools in your security arsenal, acting as virtual gatekeepers that control inbound and outbound traffic to your cloud resources.

Security Groups:

Security groups act as virtual firewalls for your cloud instances, such as virtual machines (VMs) or containers. They provide a stateful layer of security at the instance level, allowing you to define rules that control inbound and outbound traffic based on factors like source IP address, destination port, and protocol.

Key Characteristics of Security Groups:

- **Instance-Level Protection:** Security groups are associated with individual instances, providing granular control over traffic to and from each instance.
- **Stateful Filtering:** Security groups maintain state, meaning that return traffic is automatically allowed if the initial outbound traffic was permitted.
- **Rule-Based:** Security groups operate based on rules that you define, specifying allowed traffic based on source, destination, port, and protocol.
- **Default Deny:** All traffic is denied by default unless explicitly allowed by a rule, ensuring a secure baseline.
- **Directionality:** Rules can be applied to inbound or outbound traffic, providing flexibility in controlling traffic flow.

Firewalls:

Firewalls are network security devices that monitor and control incoming and outgoing network traffic based on predetermined security rules. They act as a barrier between your internal network and external networks, such as the internet, preventing unauthorized access and malicious activity.

Types of Firewalls:

- **Network Firewalls:** Operate at the network level, inspecting traffic based on IP addresses, ports, and protocols.
- **Host-Based Firewalls:** Run on individual hosts, providing protection at the operating system level.
- **Web Application Firewalls (WAFs):** Specialized firewalls that protect web applications from attacks like SQL injection and cross-site scripting (XSS).

How Security Groups and Firewalls Work Together:

Security groups and firewalls complement each other to provide comprehensive network security. Security groups provide instance-level protection, while firewalls offer broader network-level protection.

Benefits of Security Groups and Firewalls:

- **Enhanced Security:** Protect your cloud resources from unauthorized access and malicious attacks.
- **Granular Control:** Define fine-grained rules to control traffic flow based on various criteria.
- **Network Segmentation:** Segment your network into isolated sections to limit the impact of security breaches.
- **Compliance:** Meet regulatory compliance requirements by implementing appropriate security controls.
- **Peace of Mind:** Gain confidence in the security of your cloud infrastructure.

Best Practices for Security Groups and Firewalls:

- **Principle of Least Privilege:** Allow only the necessary traffic and restrict all other traffic by default.
- **Regular Reviews:** Regularly review and update your security group rules and firewall configurations to adapt to changing needs and threats.
- **Defense in Depth:** Implement multiple layers of security, combining security groups, firewalls, and other security measures for comprehensive protection.

- **Monitoring and Logging:** Monitor network traffic and security logs to identify and respond to potential security incidents.

Security Group and Firewall Services in the Cloud:

Cloud providers offer a variety of security group and firewall services to protect your cloud resources:

- **AWS:** Security Groups, AWS Network Firewall, AWS WAF
- **Azure:** Network Security Groups (NSGs), Azure Firewall, Azure WAF
- **GCP:** Firewall Rules, Google Cloud Armor

Conclusion:

Security groups and firewalls are essential components of cloud security, providing a robust defense against unauthorized access and malicious attacks. By understanding their capabilities and implementing best practices, you can effectively protect your cloud resources and maintain a secure and compliant cloud environment.

Part III: Building Cloud Applications with Python

Chapter 7: Introduction to Web Frameworks

Flask: A Microframework for Web Development

In the world of web development, frameworks provide a structured and efficient way to build web applications. Flask, a microframework for Python, stands out for its simplicity, flexibility, and ease of use. It provides the essential tools you need to create web applications without imposing rigid structures or unnecessary complexities.

What is a Microframework?

A microframework is a minimalistic web framework that provides only the core components needed for web development. Unlike full-fledged frameworks that come with a plethora of features and opinions, microframeworks offer a lean and flexible foundation, allowing developers to choose and integrate additional components as needed.

Key Features of Flask:

- **Lightweight and Minimalistic:** Flask has a small core and minimal dependencies, making it easy to learn and use.
- **Flexibility:** Flask gives you the freedom to choose the tools and libraries you want to use, allowing you to tailor your development environment to your specific needs.
- **WSGI Compliance:** Flask is compliant with the Web Server Gateway Interface (WSGI) standard, ensuring compatibility with various web servers.
- **Jinja2 Templating:** Flask uses the Jinja2 templating engine, providing a powerful and flexible way to generate dynamic HTML pages.
- **URL Routing:** Flask's routing system allows you to define clean and flexible URLs for your web application.
- **Easy to Extend:** Flask can be easily extended with various extensions that provide additional functionalities like database integration, form handling, and user authentication.

Benefits of Using Flask:

- **Simplicity:** Flask's minimalistic design makes it easy to learn and use, even for beginners.

- **Flexibility:** Flask gives you the freedom to choose the tools and libraries you want to use, allowing you to tailor your development environment to your specific needs.
- **Control:** Flask gives you more control over your application's structure and design compared to full-fledged frameworks.
- **Scalability:** Flask can be used to build scalable web applications, although it may require more manual configuration compared to full-fledged frameworks.
- **Great for Small to Medium-Sized Projects:** Flask is particularly well-suited for small to medium-sized projects where a full-fledged framework might be overkill.

When to Choose Flask:

Flask is a great choice for:

- **Small to medium-sized projects:** Flask's lightweight design makes it ideal for projects where a full-fledged framework might be unnecessary.
- **Prototyping and experimentation:** Flask's flexibility allows you to quickly prototype and experiment with different ideas.

- **RESTful APIs:** Flask is well-suited for building RESTful APIs due to its simplicity and flexibility.
- **Microservices:** Flask's lightweight design makes it a good choice for building microservices.

Getting Started with Flask:

To get started with Flask, you can install it using pip and follow the official Flask tutorial to create your first web application. Flask's excellent documentation and active community provide ample resources for learning and troubleshooting.

Conclusion:

Flask is a versatile and user-friendly microframework that empowers you to build web applications with ease. Its simplicity, flexibility, and control make it a popular choice for developers who value a minimalistic approach to web development.

Django: A High-Level Framework for Complex Applications

While Flask provides a minimalist approach to web development, Django takes a more comprehensive "batteries-included" approach. Django is a high-level Python web framework that encourages rapid development and clean, pragmatic design. It provides a robust set of tools and features for building complex, data-driven web applications, taking care of many common web development tasks so you can focus on writing your app without reinventing the wheel.

Key Features of Django:

- **Object-Relational Mapper (ORM):** Django's ORM provides an abstraction layer over your database, allowing you to interact with your database using Python code instead of writing raw SQL queries. This simplifies database interactions and makes your code more portable across different database systems.
- **Template Engine:** Django's template engine allows you to separate the presentation layer (HTML) from the business logic, making your code cleaner and easier to maintain.
- **URL Routing:** Django's URL routing system allows you to define clean and flexible URLs for your web application.
- **Admin Interface:** Django provides a built-in admin interface that allows you to easily manage your application's data.
- **Security:** Django takes security seriously, providing built-in protection against common

web vulnerabilities like cross-site scripting (XSS), cross-site request forgery (CSRF), and SQL injection.[1]

- **Scalability:** Django is designed to be scalable, allowing you to handle high traffic volumes and growing data needs.

Django's MTV Architecture:

Django follows the Model-Template-View (MTV) architectural pattern, which is a variation of the Model-View-Controller (MVC) pattern.

- **Model:** Represents your application's data structure, typically defined as Python classes that map to database tables.
- **Template:** Defines the presentation layer of your application, using Django's template language to generate dynamic HTML.
- **View:** Handles the logic of your application, processing user requests, interacting with the model, and rendering templates.

Benefits of Using Django:

- **Rapid Development:** Django's "batteries-included" approach and built-in features accelerate development, allowing you to build web applications quickly and efficiently.

- **Clean and Maintainable Code:** Django's MTV architecture and emphasis on clean design promote code organization and maintainability.
- **Security:** Django's built-in security features protect your application from common web vulnerabilities.
- **Scalability:** Django's architecture and optimizations enable you to handle high traffic volumes and growing data needs.
- **Large Community and Ecosystem:** Django has a vibrant and active community, providing ample resources, support, and third-party packages.

When to Choose Django:

Django is a great choice for building:

- **Complex web applications:** Django's comprehensive features and robust architecture are well-suited for building complex, data-driven applications.
- **Content management systems (CMS):** Django's ORM, template engine, and admin interface make it ideal for building custom CMS solutions.
- **E-commerce platforms:** Django's security features and scalability make it a suitable

choice for building secure and reliable e-commerce applications.

- **Social networks and community platforms:** Django's ability to handle user authentication, data relationships, and high traffic volumes makes it a good fit for social platforms.

Getting Started with Django:

To get started with Django, you can install it using pip and follow the official Django tutorial to create your first project. Django's extensive documentation and active community provide ample resources for learning and troubleshooting.

Conclusion:

Django is a powerful and versatile web framework that empowers you to build complex, data-driven web applications with ease. Its "batteries-included" approach, clean design, and focus on security and scalability make it a popular choice for developers worldwide.

FastAPI: A Modern, High-Performance Framework

In the realm of modern web development, where speed, efficiency, and developer productivity are paramount, FastAPI has emerged as a game-changer. FastAPI is a modern, high-performance web framework for building APIs with Python 3.6+ based on standard Python type hints.[1] It combines the best features of Starlette (for asynchronous performance) and Pydantic (for data validation) to deliver a truly exceptional development experience.

Key Features of FastAPI:

- **Speed:** FastAPI is one of the fastest Python web frameworks available, boasting performance on par with NodeJS and Go. This exceptional speed is attributed to its asynchronous capabilities powered by Starlette.
- **Fast to Code:** FastAPI's intuitive design and use of type hints significantly boost development speed, allowing you to build features faster with less code.
- **Fewer Bugs:** Type hints and automatic data validation help reduce human-induced errors, leading to more robust and reliable applications.
- **Intuitive:** FastAPI offers excellent editor support and completion everywhere, making coding a breeze and reducing debugging time.

- **Easy:** Designed with ease of use in mind, FastAPI is easy to learn and use, even for beginners.
- **Standards-Based:** FastAPI is based on (and fully compatible with) the open standards for APIs: OpenAPI (previously known as Swagger) and JSON Schema.[2] This ensures interoperability and allows you to leverage a wide range of tools and libraries.
- **Automatic Interactive Documentation:** FastAPI automatically generates interactive API documentation, making it easy to test and share your API with others.

Benefits of Using FastAPI:

- **High Performance:** Build blazing-fast APIs that can handle high traffic volumes and demanding workloads.
- **Increased Productivity:** Develop features faster with less code, thanks to FastAPI's intuitive design and use of type hints.
- **Reduced Errors:** Minimize bugs and errors through automatic data validation and type checking.
- **Improved Developer Experience:** Enjoy a smooth and efficient development

experience with excellent editor support and interactive documentation.

- **Easy to Learn:** FastAPI's clear and concise documentation makes it easy to learn and use, even for developers new to web frameworks.
- **Ideal for APIs:** FastAPI is particularly well-suited for building RESTful APIs, offering features like data validation, serialization, and automatic documentation.

When to Choose FastAPI:

FastAPI is a great choice for:

- **Building high-performance APIs:** When speed and efficiency are critical, FastAPI is an excellent choice.
- **Developing microservices:** FastAPI's lightweight design and focus on APIs make it ideal for building microservices.
- **Modern web applications:** FastAPI's asynchronous capabilities and support for WebSockets make it suitable for modern web applications that require real-time interactions.
- **Data science and machine learning:** FastAPI can be used to build APIs for

serving machine learning models and data science applications.

Getting Started with FastAPI:

To get started with FastAPI, you can install it using pip and follow the official FastAPI tutorial to create your first API. FastAPI's comprehensive documentation and active community provide ample resources for learning and troubleshooting.

FastAPI is a modern and powerful web framework that empowers you to build high-performance APIs with ease. Its speed, efficiency, and developer-friendly features make it a compelling choice for developers who want to build robust and scalable web applications.

Chapter 8: Developing and Deploying Web Applications

Building a Simple Web Application

Now that you've explored the foundations of web frameworks, it's time to put your knowledge into practice. In this section, we'll walk through the process of building a simple web application using Flask, a microframework known for its simplicity and flexibility. This hands-on experience will solidify your understanding of web development concepts and empower you to create your own web applications.

Project Overview:

We'll build a basic "To-Do List" application that allows users to add, view, and delete tasks. This project will demonstrate fundamental web development concepts, including:

- **Setting up a Flask development environment**
- **Defining routes and views**
- **Handling user input**
- **Rendering templates**
- **Working with a database (SQLite)**

Step 1: Setting up the Environment:

1. **Install Flask:** If you haven't already, install Flask using pip:

Bash

```bash
pip install Flask
```

2. **Create Project Structure:** Create a new project directory and a file named `app.py` within it. This file will contain our Flask application code.

Step 2: Creating the Flask App:

1. **Import Flask:** In `app.py`, import the Flask class:

Python

```python
from flask import Flask, render_template, request, redirect, url_for
```

2. **Create an App Instance:** Create an instance of the Flask class:

Python

```python
app = Flask(__name__)
```

3. **Define the Database:** We'll use SQLite for simplicity. Add the following to `app.py`:

Python

```python
import sqlite3

DATABASE = 'todo.db'

def get_db():
    db = getattr(g, '_database', None)
    if db is None:
        db = g._database = sqlite3.connect(DATABASE)
    return db

@app.teardown_appcontext
def close_connection(exception):
    db = getattr(g, '_database', None)
    if db is not None:
        db.close()
```

```
def¹ init_db():
    with app.app_context():
        db = get_db()
                                        with
app.open_resource('schema.sql',    mode='r')
as f:

db.cursor().executescript(f.read())
        db.commit()²
```

4. **Create the Database Schema:** Create a file named `schema.sql` in your project directory with the following SQL code:

SQL

```sql
DROP TABLE IF EXISTS tasks;
CREATE TABLE tasks (
    id INTEGER PRIMARY KEY AUTOINCREMENT,
    content TEXT NOT NULL
);
```

5. **Initialize the Database:** Add the following to `app.py` to initialize the database when the app starts:

Python

```
init_db()
```

Step 3: Defining Routes and Views:

1. **Index Route:** Define a route for the index page that displays the to-do list:

Python

```python
@app.route('/')
def index():
    db = get_db()
    cur = db.execute('SELECT * FROM tasks')
    tasks = cur.fetchall()
        return render_template('index.html',
tasks=tasks)
```

2. **Add Task Route:** Define a route to handle adding new tasks:

Python

```python
@app.route('/add', methods=['POST'])
def add():
    content = request.form['content']
```

```
    db = get_db()
    db.execute('INSERT INTO tasks (content)
VALUES (?)', (content,))
    db.commit()
    return redirect(url_for('index'))
```

3. **Delete Task Route:** Define a route to handle deleting tasks:

Python

```
@app.route('/delete/<int:task_id>')
def delete(task_id):
    db = get_db()
    db.execute('DELETE FROM tasks WHERE id
= ?', (task_id,))
    db.commit()
    return redirect(url_for('index'))
```

Step 4: Creating the Template:

1. **Create a Templates Directory:** Create a directory named `templates` in your project directory.

2. **Create** `index.html`: Create a file named `index.html` within the `templates` directory with the following HTML code:

HTML

```
<!DOCTYPE html>
<html>
<head>
    <title>To-Do List</title>
</head>
<body>
    <h1>To-Do List</h1>
    <form method="POST" action="/add">
        <input type="text" name="content"[3]
placeholder="Add task...">
        <button type="submit">Add</button>
    </form>
    <ul>
        {% for task in tasks %}
                    <li>{{ task[1] }} <a
href="/delete/{{                      task[0]
}}">Delete</a></li>
        {% endfor %}
    </ul>
</body>
</html>
```

Step 5: Running the Application:

1. **Run the App:** In your terminal, run the following command from your project directory:

Bash

```
flask run
```

2. **Access the App:** Open your web browser and go to `http://127.0.0.1:5000/` to access your to-do list application.

Conclusion:

You've now built a simple web application using Flask! This example demonstrates the basic steps involved in web development, including setting up a development environment, defining routes and views, handling user input, rendering templates, and working with a database. This foundation will serve you well as you explore more complex web development projects.

Testing and Debugging

Creating a web application involves more than just writing code; it also requires ensuring that the application functions correctly and reliably. This is where testing and debugging come into play. Testing involves systematically checking your application for errors and unexpected behavior, while debugging is the process of identifying and fixing those errors.

Why Testing is Crucial:

- **Identify Errors Early:** Testing helps catch errors early in the development process, making them easier and less expensive to fix.
- **Improve Code Quality:** Testing encourages you to write cleaner, more modular code that is easier to maintain and debug.
- **Ensure Reliability:** Thorough testing increases confidence in your application's reliability and stability.
- **Enhance User Experience:** Testing helps ensure that your application meets user expectations and provides a positive user experience.

Types of Testing:

- **Unit Testing:** Testing individual components or modules of your application in isolation.
- **Integration Testing:** Testing how different components of your application work together.
- **Functional Testing:** Testing the overall functionality of your application against its requirements.
- **End-to-End Testing:** Testing the entire application flow from start to finish, simulating real user scenarios.
- **User Acceptance Testing (UAT):** Testing performed by end-users to ensure the application meets their needs and expectations.

Testing Frameworks:

Python offers several testing frameworks to help you write and execute tests:

- **unittest:** Python's built-in testing framework, providing a set of tools for writing and running tests.
- **pytest:** A popular third-party testing framework known for its simplicity and flexibility.

Debugging Techniques:

- **Print Statements:** A simple but effective way to inspect variable values and program flow.
- **Debuggers:** Tools that allow you to step through your code line by line, inspect variables, and set breakpoints.
- **Logging:** Record events and errors in a log file for analysis and troubleshooting.
- **Error Messages:** Pay close attention to error messages, which often provide clues about the cause of the error.
- **Code Review:** Have another developer review your code to identify potential issues.

Debugging Tools:

- **Python Debugger (pdb):** Python's built-in debugger.
- **IDEs with Debugging Capabilities:** Many IDEs, such as VS Code and PyCharm, offer integrated debugging tools.

Best Practices for Testing and Debugging:

- **Write Tests First:** Consider writing tests before you write code (Test-Driven Development).
- **Test Frequently:** Test your code regularly as you develop to catch errors early.

- **Use a Testing Framework:** Use a testing framework to organize and execute your tests.
- **Write Meaningful Tests:** Write tests that cover different scenarios and edge cases.
- **Use a Debugger:** Use a debugger to step through your code and identify the root cause of errors.
- **Log Effectively:** Use logging to record events and errors for analysis.
- **Read Error Messages Carefully:** Pay attention to error messages and use them to guide your debugging efforts.

Conclusion:

Testing and debugging are essential practices in web development, ensuring that your applications are reliable, functional, and user-friendly. By incorporating testing and debugging techniques into your development workflow, you can improve code quality, reduce errors, and deliver a better user experience.

Deployment to the Cloud

8.3 Deployment to the Cloud

Developing a web application is only half the battle; making it accessible to users worldwide is the ultimate goal. This involves deploying your application to the cloud, where it can leverage the scalability, reliability, and global reach of cloud infrastructure. In this section, we'll explore the process of deploying your Flask application to Heroku, a popular cloud platform that simplifies web app deployment.

Why Deploy to the Cloud?

- **Accessibility:** Make your application accessible to users worldwide, 24/7.
- **Scalability:** Handle traffic spikes and growing user demand with ease.
- **Reliability:** Leverage the redundancy and fault tolerance of cloud infrastructure.
- **Cost-Efficiency:** Reduce infrastructure costs and pay only for the resources you use.
- **Simplified Management:** Offload server management and maintenance to the cloud provider.

Choosing a Cloud Platform:

Several cloud platforms cater to web application deployment, each with its strengths and features:

- **Heroku:** A platform-as-a-service (PaaS) provider known for its ease of use and developer-friendly tools.
- **AWS Elastic Beanstalk:** AWS's PaaS offering for deploying and scaling web applications and services.
- **Azure App Service:** Microsoft's PaaS solution for hosting web applications, REST APIs, and mobile backends.
- **Google App Engine:** GCP's fully managed serverless platform for web applications and APIs.

Deploying to Heroku:

Heroku simplifies web application deployment, allowing you to focus on your code rather than server configuration. Here's a general outline of the deployment process:

1. Prepare Your Application:

- **Requirements File:** Create a `requirements.txt` file listing your application's dependencies. This ensures Heroku installs the necessary packages.

Bash

```
pip freeze > requirements.txt
```

- **Procfile:** Create a `Procfile` (no file extension) to specify the commands that start your application. For a Flask app, it might look like this:

```
web: gunicorn app:app
```

- (Note: You'll need to install `gunicorn`: `pip install gunicorn`)
- **WSGI File:** If your app's entry point isn't named `app.py` or the Flask app instance isn't named `app`, you'll need a WSGI file (e.g., `wsgi.py`) to tell Heroku where to find your app. Example:

Python

```
from myapp import myapp as application
```

- **Static Files:** If your application uses static files (CSS, JavaScript, images), create a `static` folder within your app directory.

2. Create a Heroku Account and Install the Heroku CLI:

- **Sign Up:** Sign up for a free Heroku account at heroku.com.
- **Install CLI:** Install the Heroku Command Line Interface (CLI) to interact with Heroku from your terminal.

3. Initialize a Git Repository and Deploy:

- **Git Init:** Initialize a Git repository in your project directory:

Bash

```
git init
```

- **Heroku Login:** Log in to Heroku through the CLI:

Bash

```
heroku login
```

- **Create Heroku App:** Create a new Heroku application:

Bash

```
heroku create
```

- **Deploy:** Deploy your code to Heroku using Git:

Bash

```
git add .
git commit -m "Initial deployment"
git push heroku master
```

4. Database Setup (if applicable):

If your application uses a database, you'll need to provision a database add-on on Heroku. Heroku offers various database options, including PostgreSQL, MySQL, and Redis.

5. Scaling and Monitoring:

Heroku provides tools for scaling your application by adding more dynos (lightweight Linux containers that run your application) and monitoring its performance and resource usage.

Deploying your web application to the cloud opens up a world of possibilities, allowing you to reach a global audience and leverage the scalability and reliability of cloud infrastructure. Heroku provides a user-friendly platform for deploying and managing your Flask applications, simplifying the deployment process and allowing you to focus on building great web experiences.

Chapter 9: APIs and Microservices

Creating RESTful APIs with Python

In today's interconnected digital landscape, Application Programming Interfaces (APIs) serve as the crucial bridges that allow different software systems to communicate and interact with each other. RESTful APIs, in particular, have become the dominant architectural style for web APIs, offering a standardized and flexible approach to building web services. This section guides you through the process of creating RESTful APIs using Python and the Flask framework.

What are RESTful APIs?

REST (Representational State Transfer) is an architectural style for designing networked applications. It leverages the existing infrastructure and protocols of the World Wide Web, primarily HTTP, to define a set of constraints and principles for creating web services. RESTful APIs adhere to these principles, providing a standardized and flexible way for different applications to exchange data.

Key Principles of REST:

- **Client-Server Architecture:** Separates the concerns of the client (the consumer of the API) and the server (the provider of the API).
- **Statelessness:** Each request from the client to the server must contain all the information necessary to understand and process the request.[1]
- **Cacheability:** Responses from the server should explicitly state whether they can be cached or not, improving performance and scalability.
- **Uniform Interface:** Defines a consistent interface for interacting with the API, including the use of standard HTTP methods (GET, POST, PUT, DELETE) and resource identifiers (URIs).
- **Layered System:** Allows for the layering of system components, such as security layers or caching layers, without the client needing to know the internal details of the server.
- **Code on Demand (optional):** Allows the server to send executable code to the client, extending or customizing the client's functionality.

Building a RESTful API with Flask:

Flask, with its simplicity and flexibility, provides an excellent foundation for building RESTful APIs.

Here's a basic example of creating a simple API for managing a to-do list:

Python

```python
from flask import Flask, request, jsonify

app = Flask(__name__)

tasks = [
    {
        'id': 1,
        'content': 'Buy groceries',
        'done': False
    },
    {
        'id': 2,
        'content': 'Learn Python',
        'done': False
    }
]

@app.route('/tasks', methods=['GET'])
def get_tasks():
    return jsonify({'tasks': tasks})

@app.route('/tasks/<int:task_id>',
methods=['GET'])
def get_task(task_id):
    task = [task for task in tasks if task['id'] == task_id]
    if len(task) == 0:
```

```python
        return jsonify({'message': 'Task
not found'}),² 404
    return jsonify({'task': task[0]})


@app.route('/tasks', methods=['POST'])
def create_task():
    if not request.json or not 'content' in
request.json:
        return jsonify({'message': 'Missing
content'}), 400
    task = {
        'id': tasks[-1]['id'] + 1,
        'content': request.json['content'],
        'done': False
    }
    tasks.append(task)
    return jsonify({'task': task}), 201


@app.route('/tasks/<int:task_id>',
methods=['PUT'])
def update_task(task_id):
    task = [task for task in tasks if
task['id'] == task_id]
    if len(task) == 0:³
        return jsonify({'message': 'Task
not found'}),⁴ 404
    if not request.json:
        return jsonify({'message': 'No data
provided'}), 400
                task[0]['content']    =
request.json.get('content',
task[0]['content'])
```

```
                 task[0]['done']        =
request.json.get('done', task[0]['done'])
    return jsonify({'task': task[0]})

@app.route('/tasks/<int:task_id>',
methods=['DELETE'])
def delete_task(task_id):
    task = [task for task in tasks if
task['id'] == task_id]
    if len(task)⁵ == 0:
        return jsonify({'message': 'Task
not found'}),⁶ 404
    tasks.remove(task[0])
        return jsonify({'message': 'Task
deleted'}), 200

if __name__ == '__main__':
    app.run(debug=True)
```

Explanation:

- This code defines a Flask application with
  several routes (`/tasks`,
  `/tasks/<int:task_id>`) that handle different
  HTTP methods (GET, POST, PUT, DELETE)
  for managing tasks.

146

- The `jsonify` function is used to convert Python dictionaries to JSON format for API responses.
- Different HTTP status codes (200 OK, 201 Created, 400 Bad Request, 404 Not Found) are used to indicate the success or failure of requests.

Key Considerations for RESTful API Development:

- **Resource Design:** Carefully design your resources (e.g., tasks, users, products) and their associated URIs.
- **HTTP Methods:** Utilize the appropriate HTTP methods (GET, POST, PUT, DELETE) for different actions on resources.
- **Status Codes:** Use meaningful HTTP status codes to indicate the success or failure of requests.
- **Data Format:** Choose a suitable data format for exchanging information, typically JSON or XML.
- **Error Handling:** Implement proper error handling to provide informative error messages to clients.
- **Documentation:** Document your API clearly and concisely to facilitate client integration.

Tools and Libraries:

Several tools and libraries can assist in RESTful API development with Python:

- **Flask-RESTful:** An extension for Flask that simplifies the creation of RESTful APIs.
- **Marshmallow:** A library for object serialization and deserialization, useful for converting objects to and from JSON or other formats.
- **Swagger/OpenAPI:** A specification and framework for describing RESTful APIs, enabling automatic documentation generation and client SDK creation.

Creating RESTful APIs with Python and Flask empowers you to build web services that can be consumed by various applications. By adhering to REST principles and utilizing the appropriate tools and libraries, you can create well-designed, robust, and scalable APIs that facilitate seamless communication between different software systems.

Consuming APIs in Your Applications

While creating APIs enables your applications to expose functionalities and data to others, consuming APIs allows your applications to leverage external services and data sources. This opens up a world of possibilities, allowing you to integrate third-party features, access valuable data, and build richer and more powerful applications. In this section, we'll explore how to consume APIs in your Python applications using the `requests` library.

What is API Consumption?

API consumption refers to the process of accessing and interacting with an API provided by another application or service. This involves sending requests to the API endpoints and processing the responses received.

The `requests` Library:

The `requests` library is a powerful and user-friendly Python library for making HTTP requests. It simplifies the process of interacting with web services, providing an intuitive interface for sending requests and handling responses.

Making API Requests:

Here's a basic example of how to use the `requests` library to make a GET request to a public API:

Python

```
import requests
```

```
response                              =
requests.get('https://api.example.com/data'
)

print(response.status_code)    # Check the
status code (e.g., 200 OK)
print(response.json())    # Access the JSON
response data
```

Explanation:

- This code imports the `requests` library and
  uses the `get()` method to send a GET
  request to the specified API endpoint.
- The `response` object contains information
  about the API response, including the status
  code and the response data.
- The `json()` method is used to parse the
  JSON response data into a Python
  dictionary.

Handling Different HTTP Methods:

The `requests` library supports various HTTP
methods, including:

- `GET`: Retrieve data from the API.

- POST: Send data to the API to create a new resource.
- PUT: Send data to the API to update an existing resource.
- DELETE: Request the API to delete a resource.

Example using POST:

Python

```
import requests

data = {'name': 'John Doe', 'email': 'john.doe@example.com'}

response = requests.post('https://api.example.com/users', json=data)

print(response.status_code)
print(response.json())
```

Handling API Responses:

- **Status Codes:** Check the response status code to determine the success or failure of the request.

- **Data Parsing:** Parse the response data according to its format (e.g., JSON, XML).
- **Error Handling:** Implement error handling to gracefully handle API errors and exceptions.

Authentication:

Many APIs require authentication to access their resources. Common authentication methods include:

- **API Keys:** Unique keys provided to identify and authenticate clients.
- **OAuth:** An open standard for authorization, allowing users to grant access to their resources without sharing their credentials.

API Documentation:

Always refer to the API documentation for details on:

- **Endpoints:** The URLs for accessing different resources.
- **Methods:** The supported HTTP methods for each endpoint.
- **Request Parameters:** The required or optional parameters for API requests.
- **Response Format:** The format of the API responses (e.g., JSON, XML).

- **Authentication:** The authentication methods required to access the API.

Best Practices for API Consumption:

- **Error Handling:** Implement robust error handling to gracefully handle API errors and exceptions.
- **Rate Limiting:** Respect API rate limits to avoid being blocked or throttled.
- **Caching:** Cache frequently accessed data to improve performance and reduce API calls.
- **Security:** Handle sensitive data (e.g., API keys, user credentials) securely.

Consuming APIs in your Python applications allows you to leverage external services and data sources, enriching your applications and expanding their capabilities. By understanding API consumption principles, utilizing the `requests` library, and following best practices, you can seamlessly integrate with external APIs and build more powerful and feature-rich applications.

Building Microservices-Based Architectures

In the ever-evolving landscape of software development, microservices have emerged as a powerful architectural pattern for building complex and scalable applications. Unlike traditional monolithic architectures, where all components are tightly coupled within a single codebase, microservices break down applications into small, independent services that communicate with each other. This modular approach offers numerous benefits in terms of agility, scalability, and resilience.

What are Microservices?

Microservices are small, autonomous services that work together to form a larger application. Each microservice focuses on a specific business capability and can be developed, deployed, and scaled independently. This[1] allows for greater flexibility, agility, and resilience compared to monolithic architectures.

Key Characteristics of Microservices:

- **Small and Focused:** Each microservice is responsible for a specific business function.
- **Autonomous:** Microservices can be developed, deployed, and scaled independently.
- **Loosely Coupled:** Microservices communicate with each other through well-defined APIs, minimizing dependencies.

- **Technology Diversity:** Different microservices can be built using different technologies and programming languages.
- **Decentralized Governance:** Teams have autonomy in choosing the technologies and tools for their microservices.

Benefits of Microservices:

- **Increased Agility:** Develop, deploy, and scale individual services independently, enabling faster release cycles and quicker response to changing requirements.
- **Improved Scalability:** Scale individual services independently based on their specific needs, optimizing resource utilization and cost efficiency.
- **Enhanced Resilience:** Isolate failures to individual services, preventing cascading failures and improving overall application stability.
- **Technology Diversity:** Use the best technology for each service, allowing you to leverage different programming languages, frameworks, and databases.
- **Team Autonomy:** Empower teams to work independently and make their own technology choices, fostering innovation and ownership.

Challenges of Microservices:

- **Increased Complexity:** Managing a distributed system of microservices can be more complex than managing a monolithic application.
- **Inter-Service Communication:** Designing and managing communication between microservices requires careful consideration.
- **Data Consistency:** Maintaining data consistency across multiple microservices can be challenging.
- **Testing and Debugging:** Testing and debugging a distributed system can be more complex than testing a monolithic application.
- **Deployment and Monitoring:** Deploying and monitoring a large number of microservices requires robust infrastructure and tools.

Building Microservices with Python:

Python, with its versatility and rich ecosystem of libraries and frameworks, is well-suited for building microservices. Flask and FastAPI, in particular, are popular choices for creating lightweight and efficient microservices.

Key Considerations for Microservice Development:

- **API Design:** Design clear and well-defined APIs for communication between microservices.
- **Data Management:** Choose appropriate data storage solutions for each microservice, considering factors like data consistency and scalability.
- **Service Discovery:** Implement a service discovery mechanism to allow microservices to locate each other dynamically.
- **Communication Patterns:** Choose appropriate communication patterns, such as synchronous request-response or asynchronous messaging.
- **Fault Tolerance:** Implement fault tolerance mechanisms to handle service failures gracefully.
- **Monitoring and Logging:** Implement robust monitoring and logging to track service performance and identify issues.

Tools and Technologies:

- **Docker:** Containerize microservices for portability and consistency.

- **Kubernetes:** Orchestrate and manage containerized microservices.
- **API Gateways:** Provide a single entry point for clients to access microservices.
- **Message Queues:** Enable asynchronous communication between microservices.
- **Service Meshes:** Manage and monitor communication between microservices.

Microservices offer a powerful architectural approach for building complex and scalable applications. By breaking down applications into small, independent services, you can achieve greater agility, scalability, and resilience. Python, with its versatility and rich ecosystem, provides an excellent platform for building microservices. By understanding the principles of microservice development and utilizing the appropriate tools and technologies, you can create robust and scalable microservices-based architectures.

Part IV: Advanced Topics and Best Practices

Chapter 10: Securing Your Cloud Applications

Authentication and Authorization

In the realm of cloud computing, where applications and data reside in a shared and interconnected environment, security is of paramount importance. Authentication and authorization are two fundamental pillars of cloud security, ensuring that only authorized users can access your applications and data. Authentication verifies the identity of users, while authorization determines what actions they are permitted to perform.

Authentication: Verifying User Identity

Authentication is the process of verifying the identity of a user who is attempting to access your application. It ensures that users are who they claim to be, preventing unauthorized access and protecting your sensitive data.

Common Authentication Methods:

- **Username and Password:** The most common authentication method, where users provide a unique username and a secret password to prove their identity.

- **Multi-Factor Authentication (MFA):** Adds an extra layer of security by requiring users to provide multiple factors for authentication,[1] such as something they know (password), something they have (security token), or something they are (biometric verification).
- **Social Login:** Allows users to authenticate using their existing social media accounts, such as Google, Facebook, or Twitter.
- **SAML (Security Assertion Markup Language):** An XML-based standard for exchanging authentication and authorization data between[2] different systems, often used in enterprise environments.
- **OpenID Connect (OIDC):** A simple identity layer on top of the OAuth 2.0 protocol, providing a standardized way for users to authenticate with web applications.

Authorization: Granting Access Permissions

Authorization is the process of determining what actions an authenticated user is permitted to perform within your application. It ensures that users have the appropriate access rights to resources and prevents them from accessing or modifying data they are not authorized to.

Authorization Mechanisms:

- **Role-Based Access Control (RBAC):** Assigns permissions to users based on their roles within the organization.
- **Attribute-Based Access Control (ABAC):** Defines access permissions based on attributes of users, resources, and the environment.
- **Access Control Lists (ACLs):** Lists that specify which users or groups have access to specific resources.
- **OAuth 2.0 Scopes:** Define the specific permissions that an application can request from a user, such as access to their profile information or the ability to post on their behalf.

Implementing Authentication and Authorization in Cloud Applications:

Cloud providers offer various services and tools to help you implement authentication and authorization in your applications:

- **AWS Identity and Access Management (IAM):** Provides fine-grained access control for AWS services and resources.

- **Azure Active Directory:** Microsoft's cloud-based identity and access management service.
- **Google Cloud Identity and Access Management (IAM):** Offers identity and access management for GCP resources.

Best Practices for Authentication and Authorization:

- **Strong Passwords:** Enforce strong password policies and encourage users to use unique passwords for different accounts.
- **Multi-Factor Authentication:** Implement MFA whenever possible to add an extra layer of security.
- **Principle of Least Privilege:** Grant users only the necessary permissions to perform their tasks.
- **Regular Reviews:** Regularly review and update user permissions to ensure they are still appropriate.
- **Secure Storage of Credentials:** Store user credentials securely, using techniques like hashing and encryption.
- **Session Management:** Implement secure session management to protect user sessions from hijacking.

Conclusion:

Authentication and authorization are critical components of cloud application security, ensuring that only authorized users can access your applications and data. By implementing robust authentication and authorization mechanisms, you can protect your sensitive data, prevent unauthorized access, and maintain the integrity of your cloud environment.

Data Encryption and Protection

In the cloud computing landscape, where data resides on shared infrastructure and traverses diverse networks, safeguarding sensitive information is paramount. Data encryption serves as a critical line of defense, transforming your data into an unreadable format that can only be deciphered with the appropriate decryption key. This ensures that even if unauthorized access occurs, your data remains confidential and protected.

What is Data Encryption?

Data encryption is the process of converting plaintext data into ciphertext, a form that is unreadable without the proper decryption key. This process employs cryptographic algorithms to scramble the data, rendering it unintelligible to anyone who doesn't possess the key.

Types of Encryption:

- **Symmetric Encryption:** Uses the same key for both encryption and decryption. This method is efficient for encrypting large amounts of data but requires secure key distribution. (Examples: AES, DES)
- **Asymmetric Encryption:** Uses a pair of keys: a public key for encryption and a private key for decryption. This method is ideal for secure communication and key exchange but is computationally more expensive than symmetric encryption. (Examples: RSA, ECC)

Encryption in the Cloud:

Cloud providers offer various encryption services and mechanisms to protect your data:

- **Data at Rest:** Encrypting data stored on cloud storage, databases, and other storage media.
- **Data in Transit:** Encrypting data transmitted over networks, such as between your application and the cloud provider or between different cloud services.

- **Client-Side Encryption:** Encrypting data on the client-side before it is sent to the cloud, providing an additional layer of security.
- **Server-Side Encryption:** Encrypting data on the server-side by the cloud provider, managing the encryption keys and providing security controls.

Key Management:

Proper key management is crucial for the effectiveness of encryption. Cloud providers offer key management services that allow you to create, store, and manage your encryption keys securely:

- **AWS Key Management Service (KMS):** Provides a centralized service for creating and managing encryption keys.
- **Azure Key Vault:** A secure cloud service for storing and managing secrets, including encryption keys, passwords, and certificates.
- **Google Cloud Key Management Service (KMS):** Offers a secure and centralized service for managing cryptographic keys.

Data Protection Best Practices:

- **Encrypt Sensitive Data:** Encrypt all sensitive data, including personally identifiable information (PII), financial data, and healthcare data.

- **Use Strong Encryption Algorithms:** Employ strong and well-vetted encryption algorithms, such as AES-256.
- **Secure Key Management:** Store and manage your encryption keys securely, utilizing key management services provided by your cloud provider.
- **Regular Key Rotation:** Rotate your encryption keys periodically to minimize the impact of potential key compromise.
- **Data Masking and Tokenization:** Consider data masking or tokenization techniques to protect sensitive data in non-production environments.
- **Access Control:** Implement strong access control mechanisms to limit access to sensitive data and encryption keys.
- **Data Loss Prevention (DLP):** Implement DLP solutions to prevent sensitive data from leaving your organization's control.

Compliance and Regulations:

Various compliance and regulatory requirements mandate data encryption and protection, such as:

- **General Data Protection Regulation (GDPR):** Requires organizations to implement appropriate technical and organizational measures to protect personal data.
- **Health Insurance Portability and Accountability Act (HIPAA):** Mandates the protection of patient health information (PHI).
- **Payment Card Industry Data Security Standard (PCI DSS):** Requires organizations that handle credit card information to implement security controls, including encryption.

Data encryption and protection are essential aspects of cloud security, safeguarding your sensitive information from unauthorized access and breaches. By implementing robust encryption mechanisms, employing secure key management practices, and adhering to compliance requirements, you can ensure the confidentiality and integrity of your data in the cloud.

Security Best Practices

Securing your cloud applications is an ongoing process that requires a multi-faceted approach. While authentication, authorization, and encryption are crucial components, implementing comprehensive security best practices is essential to safeguard your applications and data from evolving threats and vulnerabilities.

1. Principle of Least Privilege:

Grant users and services only the minimum necessary permissions to perform their tasks. This limits the potential damage from compromised accounts or insider threats.

2. Secure Configuration:

Properly configure your cloud services and resources, disabling unnecessary features and ensuring that security settings are up-to-date. Regularly review and update configurations as needed.

3. Vulnerability Management:

Regularly scan your applications and infrastructure for vulnerabilities, using automated tools and manual assessments. Promptly patch and remediate any identified vulnerabilities.

4. Security Monitoring and Logging:

Implement comprehensive monitoring and logging to track activity within your cloud environment.

Analyze logs to detect suspicious behavior and potential security incidents.

5. Network Security:

Secure your network infrastructure by implementing firewalls, intrusion detection systems (IDS), and other network security measures. Segment your network to isolate sensitive data and limit the impact of breaches.

6. Data Backup and Recovery:

Regularly back up your data to a separate location or cloud service. Implement disaster recovery plans to ensure business continuity in the event of an outage or disaster.

7. Security Awareness Training:

Educate your employees about security best practices and threats, such as phishing, social engineering, and malware. Promote a security-conscious culture within your organization.

8. Incident Response Planning:

Develop an incident response plan to guide your actions in the event of a security incident. Regularly test and update your plan to ensure its effectiveness.

9. Secure Coding Practices:

Implement secure coding practices to prevent vulnerabilities in your applications. Use code analysis tools and peer reviews to identify and address potential security flaws.

10. Third-Party Risk Management:

Assess and manage the security risks associated with third-party libraries, services, and integrations. Ensure that your vendors adhere to security best practices and comply with relevant regulations.

11. Infrastructure as Code (IaC):

Utilize IaC to define and manage your cloud infrastructure in a declarative manner. This promotes consistency, reduces manual errors, and enables version control for your infrastructure configurations.

12. Continuous Security Monitoring:

Implement continuous security monitoring to detect and respond to threats in real-time. Utilize security information and event management (SIEM) tools to aggregate and analyze security logs from various sources.

Cloud-Specific Security Considerations:

- **Shared Responsibility Model:** Understand the shared responsibility model of your cloud provider, where you are responsible for securing your applications and data while the provider secures the underlying infrastructure.

- **Cloud Compliance:** Ensure that your cloud environment complies with relevant security and privacy regulations, such as GDPR, HIPAA, and PCI DSS.

- **Cloud-Native Security Tools:** Leverage cloud-native security tools and services offered by your cloud provider, such as security information and event management (SIEM) tools, intrusion detection systems (IDS), and web application firewalls (WAFs).

Conclusion:

Implementing security best practices is crucial for protecting your cloud applications and data from evolving threats and vulnerabilities. By adopting a comprehensive security approach, incorporating security into every stage of your development lifecycle, and utilizing cloud-native security tools, you can create a secure and resilient cloud environment.

Chapter 11: Scalability and Performance Optimization

Scaling Your Application for Growth

Witnessing your web application flourish and attract a growing user base is incredibly rewarding. However, this success brings the crucial challenge of ensuring your application can handle the increasing workload without faltering. This is where scalability becomes paramount. Scalability refers to an application's ability to accommodate rising traffic, data volume, and transaction rates while maintaining optimal performance. Designing and implementing a scalable architecture is essential for supporting growth and delivering a seamless user experience.

Grasping the Essence of Scalability

Scalability extends beyond simply handling more users; it encompasses the efficient management of resources to accommodate growth across various dimensions:

- **Traffic:** Effectively managing increasing numbers of concurrent users and their requests, ensuring responsiveness and avoiding overload.

- **Data:** Efficiently handling and processing growing volumes of data without compromising performance or storage capacity.
- **Transactions:** Seamlessly processing a higher rate of transactions and operations, maintaining speed and reliability.
- **Geographic Reach:** Serving users distributed across different geographic locations with minimal latency, ensuring a consistent experience regardless of location.

Strategic Approaches to Scaling:

Two primary strategies are employed to achieve scalability in applications:

- **Vertical Scaling (Scaling Up):** This approach involves increasing the resources of an existing server, such as augmenting its CPU power, memory capacity, or storage space. While simpler to implement, vertical scaling has inherent limitations in terms of maximum capacity and can introduce a single point of failure.
- **Horizontal Scaling (Scaling Out):** This approach involves adding more servers to

the infrastructure to distribute the workload across multiple machines. Horizontal scaling offers greater scalability and resilience compared to vertical scaling, but it necessitates careful design and management of the distributed system.

Leveraging the Cloud for Scalability:

Cloud computing provides an inherently flexible and scalable infrastructure for web applications. Cloud providers offer a variety of services and tools specifically designed to facilitate scaling:

- **Load Balancing:** Distributes incoming traffic intelligently across multiple servers, preventing overload on any single server and ensuring high availability.
- **Auto Scaling:** Dynamically adjusts the number of servers in response to real-time demand, optimizing resource utilization and cost efficiency by scaling resources up or down as needed.
- **Caching:** Strategically stores frequently accessed data in a cache, reducing the load on the underlying database and significantly improving response times for users.
- **Content Delivery Networks (CDNs):** Distributes static content, such as images,

videos, CSS, and JavaScript files, to servers located closer to users geographically, minimizing latency and enhancing performance.

- **Database Scaling:** Cloud providers offer diverse database scaling solutions, including read replicas, sharding, and distributed databases, to accommodate growing data volumes and query loads.

Scaling Your Flask Application:

While Flask is inherently a microframework, it can be effectively scaled to handle substantial traffic with appropriate architectural design and the utilization of cloud services. Here are key considerations for scaling your Flask application:

- **Robust WSGI Server:** Employ a production-ready WSGI server like Gunicorn or uWSGI to handle multiple concurrent requests efficiently, ensuring responsiveness and stability under load.
- **Load Balancing:** Deploy your Flask application on multiple servers and utilize a load balancer to distribute incoming traffic evenly, preventing overload and ensuring high availability.

- **Strategic Caching:** Implement caching mechanisms to store frequently accessed data in a cache, reducing the load on the database and improving response times for users.
- **Scalable Database Solutions:** Choose a database solution that can scale effectively with your application's growth, such as a cloud-managed relational database or a NoSQL database, depending on your data needs.
- **Asynchronous Task Handling:** Utilize asynchronous task queues like Celery to offload long-running tasks, preventing them from blocking the main application thread and improving responsiveness.

Performance Optimization Techniques:

Beyond scaling, optimizing your application's performance is crucial for handling growth and delivering a smooth and responsive user experience. Here are some key performance optimization techniques:

- **Code Optimization:** Write efficient and optimized code, minimizing database queries, optimizing algorithms, and reducing unnecessary computations to improve overall performance.

- **Database Optimization:** Optimize database queries by using indexes, choosing appropriate database configurations, and tuning query performance to reduce database load and improve response times.
- **Effective Caching:** Implement caching strategies to store frequently accessed data in a cache, reducing database access and improving response times for users.
- **Static File Optimization:** Optimize images by reducing their file size, minify CSS and JavaScript files to reduce their size and improve loading times, and leverage browser caching to store static assets locally on the user's machine.
- **Profiling and Monitoring:** Utilize profiling tools to identify performance bottlenecks in your application and monitor key performance metrics to track performance and identify areas for improvement.

Scaling your application for growth is essential for accommodating increasing user demand and providing a seamless and responsive user experience. By understanding scaling strategies, leveraging the scalability and flexibility of cloud services, and implementing performance optimization techniques, you can build robust and scalable web applications that can handle the challenges of growth and deliver exceptional performance.

Performance Tuning Techniques

While scaling your application infrastructure can handle increased traffic and data volume, optimizing the performance of your application code and database interactions is crucial for delivering a truly responsive and efficient user experience. Performance tuning involves identifying and addressing bottlenecks in your application to minimize latency, maximize throughput, and ensure smooth operation even under heavy load.

1. Code Optimization

- **Efficient Algorithms and Data Structures:** Choose algorithms and data structures that are well-suited to the task at hand. Analyze the time and space complexity of your code to identify areas for improvement.
- **Minimize Database Interactions:** Reduce the number of database queries by fetching data in batches, using caching mechanisms, and optimizing data access patterns.

- **Optimize Loops and Iterations:** Use efficient looping constructs and avoid unnecessary iterations. Consider using list comprehensions or generator expressions for concise and optimized iterations.
- **Profiling:** Utilize profiling tools to identify performance bottlenecks in your code. These tools can pinpoint areas where code execution takes the most time, allowing you to focus your optimization efforts.

2. Database Optimization

- **Optimize Queries:** Write efficient SQL queries, avoiding unnecessary joins, subqueries, and wildcard searches. Use `EXPLAIN` (MSSMS) or similar tools to analyze query execution plans and identify areas for improvement.
- **Indexing:** Create indexes on frequently accessed columns to speed up data retrieval. Choose appropriate index types based on your query patterns.
- **Connection Pooling:** Reuse database connections to reduce the overhead of establishing new connections for each request.
- **Database Caching:** Utilize database caching mechanisms to store frequently

accessed data in memory, reducing the need to query the database repeatedly.

3. Caching Strategies

- **In-Memory Caching:** Store frequently accessed data in memory using tools like Memcached or Redis. This provides fast access to data and reduces database load.
- **Content Delivery Networks (CDNs):** Cache static content like images, videos, and CSS files on servers closer to users, reducing latency and improving loading times.
- **Browser Caching:** Leverage browser caching to store static assets locally on the user's machine, reducing the need to download them repeatedly.
- **Object Caching:** Cache frequently accessed objects or data structures in your application to avoid redundant computations or database queries.

4. Asynchronous Operations

- **Asynchronous Tasks:** Use asynchronous task queues like Celery to offload long-running tasks, such as sending emails or processing large datasets. This prevents these tasks from blocking the main application thread and improves responsiveness.

- **WebSockets:** For real-time applications, consider using WebSockets to enable bidirectional communication between the client and server, reducing latency and improving efficiency.

5. Monitoring and Performance Analysis

- **Application Performance Monitoring (APM):** Utilize APM tools to monitor your application's performance metrics, such as response times, error rates, and resource utilization.
- **Logging:** Implement logging to track application events and errors, providing insights into performance issues and potential bottlenecks.
- **Performance Testing:** Conduct performance testing to simulate real-world usage scenarios and identify performance limitations under load.

Performance Tuning for Flask Applications:

- **Gunicorn/uWSGI:** Use a production-ready WSGI server like Gunicorn or uWSGI to handle concurrent requests efficiently.

- **Caching with Flask-Caching:** Leverage Flask extensions like Flask-Caching to implement caching mechanisms in your application.
- **Database Optimization with SQLAlchemy:** Use SQLAlchemy, a powerful ORM for Python, to optimize database interactions and improve query efficiency.

Performance tuning is an iterative process that involves identifying and addressing bottlenecks in your application to optimize its speed, efficiency, and responsiveness. By employing code optimization techniques, database optimization strategies, caching mechanisms, and asynchronous operations, you can significantly enhance the performance of your web applications and deliver a seamless user experience. Remember that continuous monitoring and performance analysis are crucial for identifying areas for improvement and ensuring your application remains performant as it grows.

Load Balancing and Caching

As your web application grows and user traffic increases, ensuring its availability and responsiveness becomes critical. Load balancing and caching are two essential techniques that can significantly enhance your application's performance and scalability. Load balancing distributes incoming traffic across multiple servers, preventing overload and ensuring high availability. Caching, on the other hand, stores frequently accessed data in a readily accessible location, reducing latency and improving response times.

Load Balancing

Load balancing is the process of distributing incoming network traffic across multiple servers to prevent any single server from becoming overwhelmed. This ensures that your application remains responsive and available even under heavy load.

Benefits of Load Balancing:

- **High Availability:** If one server fails, the load balancer automatically redirects traffic to other healthy servers, preventing downtime.
- **Scalability:** Easily scale your application by adding more servers to the pool. The load balancer automatically distributes traffic to the new servers.

- **Performance:** Prevent overload on individual servers, ensuring optimal performance and responsiveness.
- **Flexibility:** Allows you to perform maintenance or upgrades on individual servers without affecting the overall availability of your application.

Load Balancing Algorithms:

Load balancers use various algorithms to distribute traffic, including:

- **Round Robin:** Distributes requests sequentially across the servers.
- **Least Connections:** Directs requests to the server with the fewest active connections.
- **IP Hash:** Routes requests based on the client's IP address, ensuring that requests from the same client are consistently sent to the same server.

Load Balancers in the Cloud:

Cloud providers offer load balancing services that integrate with their other cloud offerings:

- **AWS Elastic Load Balancing:** Provides a variety of load balancers, including

Application Load Balancers, Network Load Balancers, and Classic Load Balancers.

- **Azure Load Balancer:** Offers load balancing for applications and services deployed in Azure.
- **Google Cloud Load Balancing:** Provides global load balancing solutions for applications running on GCP.

Caching

Caching is the process of storing frequently accessed data in a cache, a temporary storage location that is closer to the user or application than the original data source. This reduces the time it takes to retrieve the data, improving performance and responsiveness.

Benefits of Caching:

- **Reduced Latency:** Retrieve data faster from the cache, reducing response times and improving user experience.
- **Reduced Database Load:** Minimize the number of queries to your database, freeing up resources and improving performance.
- **Cost Savings:** Reduce database costs by minimizing the number of queries and resource consumption.

- **Improved Scalability:** Handle increased traffic and data volume by caching frequently accessed data.

Types of Caching:

- **Browser Caching:** Store static assets (images, CSS, JavaScript) in the user's browser, reducing the need to download them repeatedly.
- **CDN Caching:** Cache content on servers geographically closer to users, improving loading times and reducing latency.
- **Server-Side Caching:** Cache data on the server-side using tools like Memcached or Redis, providing fast access to frequently accessed data.
- **Database Caching:** Utilize database caching mechanisms to store frequently accessed data in memory, reducing database load.
- **Object Caching:** Cache frequently accessed objects or data structures within your application to avoid redundant computations or database queries.

Caching Strategies:

- **Cache-Aside:** Check the cache first; if the data is not found, retrieve it from the database and store it in the cache.
- **Write-Through:** Write data to both the cache and the database simultaneously.
- **Write-Back:** Write data to the cache first and update the database asynchronously.

Caching in Flask Applications:

Flask offers extensions like Flask-Caching to simplify the implementation of caching mechanisms in your applications. You can choose from various caching backends, including Memcached, Redis, and simple in-memory caching.

Load balancing and caching are essential techniques for building scalable and performant web applications. Load balancing distributes traffic across multiple servers, ensuring high availability and preventing overload. Caching stores frequently accessed data in a readily accessible location, reducing latency and improving response times. By implementing these techniques, you can enhance your application's performance, scalability, and user experience.

Chapter 12: Monitoring and Logging

Monitoring Application Health

In the dynamic world of cloud computing, where applications are constantly interacting with users and other services, maintaining a healthy and performant system is crucial. Monitoring your application's health involves continuously tracking key metrics and indicators to gain insights into its performance, availability, and overall well-being. This proactive approach allows you to identify and address potential issues before they escalate into major problems, ensuring a smooth user experience and minimizing downtime.

Why Monitor Application Health?

- **Early Problem Detection:** Identify performance bottlenecks, errors, and anomalies before they impact users.
- **Performance Optimization:** Pinpoint areas for improvement and optimize your application for speed and efficiency.
- **Resource Utilization:** Track resource usage (CPU, memory, network) to ensure optimal allocation and cost efficiency.
- **User Experience:** Monitor user experience metrics like response times and error rates

to ensure a seamless and satisfying user journey.

- **Capacity Planning:** Anticipate future resource needs and scale your infrastructure proactively.
- **Troubleshooting:** Diagnose and resolve issues quickly by analyzing historical data and identifying trends.
- **Security Monitoring:** Detect and respond to security threats and vulnerabilities.

Key Metrics to Monitor:

- **Availability:** Track uptime and downtime to ensure your application is accessible to users.
- **Response Time:** Measure the time it takes for your application to respond to user requests.
- **Error Rate:** Monitor the frequency of errors and exceptions occurring in your application.
- **Request Rate:** Track the number of requests your application receives per second.
- **Resource Utilization:** Monitor CPU usage, memory usage, and network traffic.
- **Database Performance:** Track database query performance, connection pool usage, and database health.

- **User Activity:** Monitor user logins, page views, and other user interactions to understand usage patterns.

Monitoring Tools and Techniques:

- **Logging:** Record application events, errors, and performance data in log files for analysis and troubleshooting.
- **Application Performance Monitoring (APM) Tools:** Provide comprehensive monitoring and performance analysis capabilities, often including dashboards, alerts, and tracing.
- **Cloud Monitoring Services:** Cloud providers offer monitoring services integrated with their cloud platforms, such as AWS CloudWatch, Azure Monitor, and Google Cloud Monitoring.
- **Dashboards and Visualizations:** Create dashboards and visualizations to gain a clear and concise overview of your application's health.

Monitoring Best Practices:

- **Define Clear Objectives:** Determine what you want to achieve with your monitoring efforts and choose metrics that align with your goals.

- **Establish Baselines:** Establish baseline performance metrics to identify deviations and anomalies.
- **Set Alerts:** Configure alerts to notify you when critical metrics exceed predefined thresholds.
- **Analyze Trends:** Analyze historical data to identify trends and patterns that can help you predict future performance and resource needs.
- **Correlate Metrics:** Correlate different metrics to gain a deeper understanding of your application's behavior and identify root causes of issues.
- **Automate Monitoring:** Automate monitoring tasks to reduce manual effort and ensure continuous monitoring.

Monitoring Your Flask Application:

- **Logging with Flask:** Use Flask's built-in logging capabilities or integrate with logging libraries like `logging` to record application events and errors.
- **APM Tools:** Integrate APM tools like New Relic or Datadog to monitor your Flask application's performance.
- **Cloud Monitoring:** If you deploy your Flask application to a cloud platform, leverage the

cloud provider's monitoring services, such as AWS CloudWatch or Azure Monitor.

Conclusion:

Monitoring your application's health is essential for maintaining a performant and reliable system. By continuously tracking key metrics, utilizing monitoring tools and techniques, and following best practices, you can proactively identify and address potential issues, optimize performance, and ensure a positive user experience. Remember that monitoring is an ongoing process that requires continuous attention and adaptation to the evolving needs of your application and its users.

Logging and Troubleshooting

While monitoring provides a high-level view of your application's health, logging delves deeper, providing a detailed record of events, errors, and other relevant information that can help you diagnose and resolve issues. Logging involves capturing and storing various types of information generated by your application, creating an audit trail that can be invaluable for troubleshooting, debugging, and understanding application behavior.

Why is Logging Important?

- **Troubleshooting:** Identify the root cause of errors and exceptions by examining log entries.
- **Debugging:** Trace the execution flow of your application to pinpoint the source of bugs.
- **Auditing:** Track user actions and system events for security and compliance purposes.
- **Performance Analysis:** Analyze log data to identify performance bottlenecks and optimize your application.
- **Understanding User Behavior:** Gain insights into how users interact with your application.
- **Incident Response:** Provide valuable information for investigating and responding to security incidents.

Types of Log Data:

- **Error Logs:** Record errors and exceptions that occur during application execution.
- **Access Logs:** Track user requests and access to resources.
- **Audit Logs:** Record security-related events, such as user logins and permission changes.

- **Performance Logs:** Capture performance metrics, such as response times and database query durations.
- **Debug Logs:** Provide detailed information about the application's internal state and execution flow.

Logging Best Practices:

- **Log Meaningful Information:** Capture relevant information that can aid in troubleshooting and analysis.
- **Use Different Log Levels:** Categorize log entries by severity (e.g., debug, info, warning, error, critical) to filter and prioritize information.
- **Structure Your Logs:** Use a consistent format for log entries, including timestamps, log levels, and relevant context.
- **Centralize Logs:** Aggregate logs from different sources and servers into a central location for analysis.
- **Log Management Tools:** Utilize log management tools to collect, store, analyze, and visualize log data.
- **Retention Policies:** Define appropriate log retention policies based on compliance and business needs.

Logging in Flask Applications:

Flask provides built-in logging capabilities that you can leverage to record application events and errors. You can also integrate with logging libraries like Python's `logging` module for more advanced logging configurations.

Python

```
import logging

app.logger.setLevel(logging.DEBUG)    # Set
the logging level
app.logger.debug('This     is     a     debug
message.')
app.logger.info('This is an info message.')
app.logger.warning('This     is     a     warning
message.')
app.logger.error('This     is     an     error
message.')
app.logger.critical('This     is     a     critical
message.')[1]
```

Troubleshooting Techniques:

- **Analyze Log Files:** Examine log entries to identify errors, exceptions, and unusual patterns.

- **Use Debugging Tools:** Utilize debuggers to step through your code and inspect variables.
- **Reproduce the Issue:** Attempt to reproduce the issue in a controlled environment to gather more information.
- **Isolate the Problem:** Systematically eliminate potential causes to narrow down the source of the problem.
- **Consult Documentation:** Refer to documentation and online resources for troubleshooting tips and solutions.
- **Seek Help:** Don't hesitate to seek assistance from colleagues or online communities.

Cloud Logging Services:

Cloud providers offer logging services integrated with their cloud platforms:

- **AWS CloudWatch Logs:** Collects and stores log data from various AWS services and applications.
- **Azure Monitor Logs:** Provides log management and analysis capabilities for Azure resources.

- **Google Cloud Logging:** Collects, stores, and analyzes log data from applications and services running on GCP.

Logging and troubleshooting are essential skills for any developer or system administrator. By implementing effective logging practices and utilizing troubleshooting techniques, you can diagnose and resolve issues efficiently, maintain application stability, and ensure a positive user experience. Remember that logging is not just about recording errors; it's about capturing valuable information that can help you understand your application's behavior and optimize its performance.

Cloud Monitoring Tools

While traditional monitoring tools can be used in cloud environments, cloud providers offer specialized monitoring services that are deeply integrated with their platforms, providing a comprehensive and streamlined approach to monitoring your cloud resources and applications. These cloud monitoring tools provide valuable insights into the health, performance, and availability of your cloud infrastructure, enabling you to proactively identify and address potential issues.

Benefits of Cloud Monitoring Tools:

- **Integrated Monitoring:** Seamlessly monitor various cloud services and resources within a single platform.
- **Scalability and Performance:** Designed to handle the scale and dynamism of cloud environments, providing efficient data collection and analysis.
- **Cost-Effectiveness:** Often offered as a pay-as-you-go service, allowing you to scale your monitoring costs based on your needs.
- **Ease of Use:** Provide user-friendly interfaces and dashboards for visualizing and analyzing data.
- **Automation:** Enable automated monitoring and alerting, reducing manual effort and ensuring continuous monitoring.
- **Customization:** Allow you to tailor monitoring configurations and alerts to your specific needs.
- **Security Monitoring:** Offer features for detecting and responding to security threats and vulnerabilities.

Key Features of Cloud Monitoring Tools:

- **Data Collection:** Collect metrics, logs, and events from various cloud services and applications.
- **Metrics Monitoring:** Track key performance indicators (KPIs) such as CPU utilization, memory usage, and network traffic.
- **Log Management:** Collect, store, and analyze log data from applications and services.
- **Alerting:** Configure alerts to notify you when critical metrics exceed predefined thresholds or when specific events occur.
- **Dashboards and Visualizations:** Create customizable dashboards and visualizations to gain insights into your application's health and performance.
- **Tracing:** Trace requests across distributed systems to identify performance bottlenecks and dependencies.
- **Security Monitoring:** Detect and respond to security threats and vulnerabilities.

Popular Cloud Monitoring Tools:

- **AWS CloudWatch:** A comprehensive monitoring service for AWS resources and applications. It collects metrics, logs, and events, providing tools for alarms, dashboards, and anomaly detection.

- **Azure Monitor:** A unified monitoring platform for Azure resources and applications. It offers features for metrics, logs, alerts, dashboards, and application insights.
- **Google Cloud Monitoring:** A monitoring service for applications and services running on Google Cloud Platform. It provides features for metrics, logs, alerts, dashboards, and uptime checks.

Choosing the Right Cloud Monitoring Tool:

When selecting a cloud monitoring tool, consider factors such as:

- **Integration:** Choose a tool that integrates well with your chosen cloud platform and the services you use.
- **Features:** Select a tool that offers the features and capabilities you need, such as metrics monitoring, log management, alerting, and dashboards.
- **Scalability:** Ensure the tool can handle the scale and dynamism of your cloud environment.
- **Cost:** Evaluate the pricing model and choose a tool that aligns with your budget.

- **Ease of Use:** Select a tool with a user-friendly interface and intuitive dashboards.

Cloud monitoring tools provide a powerful and efficient way to monitor the health, performance, and availability of your cloud resources and applications. By leveraging these tools, you can gain valuable insights into your cloud environment, proactively identify and address potential issues, and ensure the smooth operation of your applications. Remember that choosing the right cloud monitoring tool is crucial for maximizing its effectiveness and aligning with your specific monitoring needs.

CONCLUSION

Congratulations! You've reached the end of your journey through the fascinating world of cloud computing with Python. Throughout this book, we've explored the fundamental concepts, essential tools, and best practices for building scalable, efficient, and secure cloud applications. You've gained valuable knowledge and practical skills that will empower you to leverage the power of the cloud for your projects, whether you're developing innovative applications, managing cloud infrastructure, or analyzing data in the cloud.

Key Takeaways:

- **Cloud Computing Fundamentals:** You've grasped the core concepts of cloud computing, its benefits, and the different service models (IaaS, PaaS, SaaS). You understand how cloud computing can transform businesses and individuals by providing on-demand access to computing resources.

- **Python for Cloud Development:** You've mastered essential Python skills for cloud development, including data types, control flow, functions, and modules. You can confidently write Python code to interact with cloud services and build cloud applications.
- **Core Cloud Services:** You've delved into the fundamental building blocks of cloud infrastructure, including compute services (VMs, containers, serverless), storage services (object storage, databases), and networking (VPCs, subnets, security). You can effectively utilize these services to build and deploy your applications.
- **Web Frameworks and APIs:** You've learned how to use popular Python web frameworks like Flask, Django, and FastAPI to create web applications and APIs. You can design and build RESTful APIs and integrate with external APIs to enhance your applications.
- **Security Best Practices:** You understand the importance of security in the cloud and have learned how to implement authentication, authorization, and encryption to protect your applications and data. You can apply security best practices to create a secure and compliant cloud environment.

- **Scalability and Performance:** You've explored techniques for scaling your applications to handle growth and optimize performance. You can leverage load balancing, caching, and other optimization strategies to ensure your applications remain responsive and efficient.
- **Monitoring and Logging:** You've learned how to monitor your applications' health, collect and analyze logs, and troubleshoot issues effectively. You can utilize cloud monitoring tools to gain insights into your applications' performance and ensure their smooth operation.

Your Capstone Project and Beyond:

As you apply the knowledge and skills you've gained from this book to your capstone project, remember that this is just the beginning of your cloud computing journey. The cloud landscape is constantly evolving, with new technologies and services emerging regularly. Embrace continuous learning, explore new tools and frameworks, and stay curious about the ever-expanding possibilities of the cloud.

A Final Note on MSSQL:

While this book covers a broad range of cloud concepts and Python techniques, remember that the core database concepts and SQL skills you've acquired are applicable across different database systems. Although specific syntax and tools might vary, the foundational knowledge you've gained will serve you well as you work with MSSQL and other database technologies.

Embrace the Cloud:

The cloud has become an integral part of the modern technology landscape, and the skills you've developed in this book are highly valuable in today's job market. Whether you're pursuing a career in cloud development, DevOps, data science, or any other field that leverages cloud computing, the knowledge and practical experience you've gained will be invaluable assets.

I encourage you to continue exploring the cloud, experimenting with new technologies, and building innovative applications that leverage the power and flexibility of this transformative technology. The future of computing is in the cloud, and you're now well-equipped to be a part of it.

www.ingramcontent.com/pod-product-compliance
Lightning Source LLC
La Vergne TN
LVHW051328050326
832903LV00031B/3417